MW01247082

That Lucky
OLD SON

RE-DISCOVERING MY FATHER THROUGH HIS WORLD WAR II BOMBER COMMAND AND POW EXPERIENCES

MARK COTE

◆ FriesenPress

Suite 300 - 990 Fort St
Victoria, BC, V8V 3K2
Canada

www.friesenpress.com

Copyright © 2018 by Mark Cote
First Edition — 2018

All rights reserved.

This is a work of creative non-fiction where some names, characters, businesses, places, events and incidents may have been altered from reality in that identifying details have been changed to protect the privacy of individuals.

No part of this publication may be reproduced in any form, or by any means, electronic or mechanical, including photocopying, recording, or any information browsing, storage, or retrieval system, without permission in writing from FriesenPress.

ISBN
978-1-5255-2036-5 (Hardcover)
978-1-5255-2037-2 (Paperback)
978-1-5255-2038-9 (eBook)

1. TRANSPORTATION, AVIATION, HISTORY

Distributed to the trade by The Ingram Book Company

www.thatluckyoldson.ca

DEDICATION

To those who served.

FOREWORD

Len Cote and I were crewmates in Bomber Command and flew several operations together (he had done many more with a previous crew). We were shot down and were prisoners together, first in *Stalag Luft VI* and then in *Stalag Luft IV*. Len had been injured when we were shot down but made light of the fact.

Mark Cote has written a book only a devoted son could write. This book reveals Len as a father and a family man as seen through Mark's eyes age five to age eight. It reveals Len's very deep belief in his Catholic religion, but most of all, it tells of his very great suffering and the attempts made by the family to relieve it.

In October 1944, a Medical Board decided that Len's injuries and illness were such that he should be included in an exchange of prisoners between the Allies and Germany. On the day of his departure, Len and I chatted for a while, said our goodbyes, and shook hands. Len turned and went to join the others who were going. I saw them go into a building in the *Vorlager*. I never saw him again.

Flight Lieutenant Douglas A. Robinson
Royal Air Force Volunteer Reserve (ret.)

AUTHOR'S NOTE

It seems that I always knew that my father flew with the Royal Air Force's Bomber Command and had spent time in a POW camp during World War II. That much, he let be known. Much of what I knew, however, was gleaned second-hand from stories that my mother and older siblings told, and from the few shreds of his service life that remained in the family: his logbook, a few certificates, and his war medals. Some time after Dad's passing, Mom had obtained for each of the seven remaining family members a copy of the book, *In Brave Company* by William Chorley and Roy Benwell when it was first published in 1977. It was one of few Bomber Command squadron histories that had been produced to that time, and although it contained many interesting first-hand accounts of the experiences of RAF 158 Squadron, I was only really interested in the few mentions of my father. Especially intriguing was the story told of his last flight, when his aircraft was shot down and he was captured. That alone irrevocably whet my appetite and created an itch to know more. But in the days before the information revolution, it seemed unlikely that I would ever have the resources to know his full story.

Over the years, however, I have gathered information, piece by piece. I have sought out every shred of detail that I could possibly obtain. I collected archival records of both my father's service and of the squadron in which he served. I read almost everything I could get my hands on about the aircraft in which he flew and the operations in which he took part. Some were gripping accounts written by veterans of those times, and some were ponderous tomes of dry fact. I also discovered that his operational squadron had formed an association of veterans, based mainly in the United Kingdom, but was also welcoming members of the Squadron veteran's families from all over the world. I joined in a heartbeat and have attended several of their annual reunions. The copious resources available from that Association led me closer to truly understanding what transpired during the war. Meeting and talking with veterans is truly sublime. Their stories brought home to me what my father may have experienced.

As my knowledge gained critical mass, it was possible to flesh out what was the likely course of his wartime experience. I could discard some information that was misrepresented or at least misunderstood. I was able to confirm other often extraordinary occurrences. There were even things I discovered that few, if any, people knew. But the question arose—what was I to do with all this information? And then my eldest sister suggested the preposterous: "You should write a book!"

I initially dismissed the idea because, for one, as a scientist, I have only ever written dry, factual material, clumsily assembled into standard formats. The last thing I wanted was for Dad's story to be a litany of facts, bereft of the feelings and emotions that must have occupied him and his colleagues during those turbulent times. I have read far too many stultifying histories of those events to ever want to add to that ballast. And so I searched for a way to bring it to life—to try to capture not just the facts, but the feelings. It was a challenge I came to relish, and in the genre of *creative non-fiction*, I may have struck the balance I sought. It is a mixture of verifiable occurrence and informed conjecture.

I have a certain gift that has served me well in this. I have a good memory for detail, occurrences, and especially conversation. Some have thought me intelligent because of it, but the truth is that I just remember stuff. It has served me well in this project because I recall very well quite a few things about my father, even if they happened or were told to me fifty years ago. It has also, I believe, allowed me to incorporate the experiences of his contemporaries, the ones to whom I have spoken, to better reflect what these men and women lived through.

And so it is to many people that I owe a debt of gratitude in being able to complete this work. Although my recollections regarding my father are vivid and rich, they likely lack the texture that maturity might have engendered. To lend context, I leaned heavily on my mother and siblings for their memories and perspective. My initial goal of this project was to tell my family what I had learned about my father. It seems now that, for much of it, they may have already known. Thank you, Bob, Lois, Elaine, Barry, and Michelle for your cherished memories and unswerving support. And thank you, Mom, for keeping Dad's love and devotion so prominent in our lives.

To my friends, I must thank you for the encouragement that you gave me. To those of you who read drafts and told me what worked and especially what didn't, I am forever grateful. Mention must go to the help, encouragement, and advice given by Cicely Robinson, Dan Durdin, David and Nanette Evans, Megan Marshall, Laura Richard, Jayda Rosenthal, Sharon Christensen, Nicola and Andrew Downes, John Robinson, Randy Widdis, Ulrike Hardenbicker, Julia Siemer, and Ron Blackwell. Your input was invaluable.

To the veterans of 158 Squadron whom I have met and whose story I have hoped to reflect in this work, I am appreciative of not only your help, but especially for your duty and service. You took the fight to the enemy at a time when it seemed hope was lost, and you and your friends paid dearly for it— many with their lives. As is reported in many an epitaph, "For your tomorrow, we gave our today." Special acknowledgement must go to Nevil "Bluey" Mottershead, Alan Bryett, Harry Irons, Donnie MacFarlane, John Cotter, and David Rosenthal. You put a human face on everything I've learned.

I cannot adequately express how much is owed to Douglas Robinson in this regard. Doug was a friend to my father and the captain of his crew. He was also a dear friend of mine. I asked him to review what I had written, and not only did he offer wise counsel and gentle corrective advice, but also unflagging encouragement throughout the process. His own story, expertly told in the self-authored book, *Life is a Great Adventure*, was also a wonderful resource for my research. There is no way I could have completed this without his generous help. Doug passed away before this book could be published. The very same week, William Noel Patterson, the other air gunner on the Robinson crew and its last surviving member also died. May that crew and all their brethren departed now stand down: their work is done.

I lastly wish to thank my dear wife, Shelley, and son, Leonard, for their patience and counsel during this long process. I truly hope that what I have assembled will make you proud.

This work is written from the perspective of those living in that period. My wish is that it purposely reflects the attitudes, feelings, and vernacular of the times and settings. The reader may find unfamiliar examples of jargon, slang, and usage. Many of these may be better understood with reference to the included glossary.

And so, I present my father's story. So many times, in discussing what my father and many like him serving in Bomber Command might have lived through, I have said, "I cannot imagine what it must have been like." And now I have attempted to do that very thing. But given the details that I know, the people I have spoken to, and knowing the person that I am (for I share my father's DNA), this is as I imagined it to have been. No one can know for certain, but I am confident that this is as close as I can reasonably get. Thank you, Dad, for all that you gave us. Your story is more than worth its telling.

INTRODUCTION

Dad was going to play records! He didn't often get a chance with the record player. Our house was home to two teenage girls, but my two elder sisters were busy with chores right now. My father had seen his chance and absconded with the appliance that normally adorned the dresser in the girls' room, beside their modest pile of phonograph discs containing the latest favourite tunes. It was the mid 1960s, and being only seven years old, I had not yet developed the sophisticated but seemingly diametrically opposed tastes independently developed by my older siblings versus that of my father. I was quite happy to enjoy both.

He had set the small, second-hand player up on the table in our living room, and I sat quietly waiting for the session to begin. I wondered if he would play his prized Johnny Horton album. I quite liked it, but tended to favour his ballads because I could always quiz my father about the historical events surrounding them. "Sink the Bismarck" was my favourite. Dad seldom mentioned his own war service, but he was not shy in discussing our side's victories in World War II.

But today he had chosen another record that I only remember him playing a few times before. It was in a plain brown sleeve and it seemed much more robust than either the small records that my sisters could afford to purchase with their meagre earnings or the few long-playing record albums that my father owned. He switched the speed of the machine to 78 rpm and the platter seemed to spin impossibly fast.

Sometimes my elder brothers would play my sisters' records at this speed. The resulting cacophony of chipmunk sounds and the inevitable pitched battle over the controls was usually quelled only by parental intervention. I wondered what would be the result of Dad's choice today. I was prepared for nearly anything.

The hiss, pops, and clicks of what was clearly a well-worn recording presaged the slow *a capella* harmony of an all-male vocal group. I would learn years later that *Les Compagnons de le Chanson* was a French group that rose to some prominence in the late 1940s and 1950s. Although they usually sang in their native tongue, Dad's record was their heavily accented English language version of "The Three Bells." The song that blared forth from the tiny speaker told the tale of the life of one Jimmy Brown. It was a simple tale of his birth, marriage, and eventual death to which his church's bell bore clarion, metaphorical witness.

"Did you like that, Son?" Dad enquired when it had finished.

Intrinsically and for reasons I would never be able to express to my father, the song made me very sad. The thought of someone dying, let alone someone singing about it, was beyond my ken at this age. I didn't want to contemplate things like that, and maybe I was a bit shocked that he would spark those feelings in me. He stood looking expectantly at me. It took some courage, but the only response I could muster was a silent but vehement shake of my head.

He just chuckled. "Maybe the other side," he said in introduction as he flipped the disk and set the tone arm.

Again, the lads started into another unaccompanied tune. Through their thick accent, I could only clearly make out the chorus, but it seemed, at first blush, to be a much lighter tune. My father, however, only stared wistfully into space while the song played.

"But dat lucky ol' sun has got nutting to do but rawl around heaven awl day ... "

I liked the sound of that. In my ignorance, I heard "son" and not "sun" and so began to picture a boy who could blissfully roam around that happy place we had always been taught we would go to in our afterlife. I might not ever understand how that "son" would get "old," but it definitely took me to a happier place than the earlier tune. I could almost imagine being that lucky old son ...

1

Dad and Mom's room was sacred ground, but it would be no match for my seven-year old ingenuity. Mom, I knew, was away at her part-time job, leaving Dad with the family. He was last seen acres away, in the living room of our small house, reading the hefty Saturday edition of the local daily. I slunk from my room past the hissing of the gas space heater in the hall and into *verboten* territory. I pondered my goal. The weathered jewellery box seemed unobtainable on top of the chest of drawers that dominated my parent's sanctuary, but my recently hatched scheme would reveal its secrets.

I tiptoed across the hardwood and carefully pulled the bottom drawer of the chest. I reckoned that standing on this improvised step would afford me enough height to peer into the hidden corners that I had only glimpsed previously. I climbed and found my target. The box opened with a barely discernible sigh, and there they were! My father's war medals! They lay in a chaotic pile of faded ribbons, silver disks, and tarnished stars crumpled unceremoniously in his corner of the modest jewellery box. I reached for one—

"What are you up to?" My father's stern voice sounded several times louder than it likely was, and I was jolted from my near-silent quest into the caught-red-handed world of reality. For a stoutly built man, he moved quite stealthily!

I knew I had to deflect the coming wrath of being found out. "What did you get those for, Daddy?" I asked, pointing at the clump of metal and cloth.

"Oh, everyone got those," he said with a dismissive wave of his hand. I learned much later that my instinctive riposte was perfect—no former airman would ever want to be accused of "shooting a line." I took what he said at face value, for I had no knowledge of what actions, experiences, or sacrifices would have led to those awards. I took advantage of my opening and considered what else was in the collection.

"What's that?" I gestured toward a tiny pair of ornately feathered silver wings attached to a small oval. It seemed insignificant in comparison to the pointy and hefty pile he had so summarily dismissed. I had pointed to his "Operational Wings" pin, a token bestowed to aircrew by the Royal Canadian Air Force to those who had completed a requisite number of sorties with Bomber Command during World War II.

"Those are my wings." he said simply, but with what I sensed was some pride and with no further explanation—as if none would ever be necessary. "Come now," he said, lifting me easily from my fashioned perch. "Your mom will be home soon."

Len hunched in his draughty coffin. His goggled eyes scanned the blackness outside of the turret of his aircraft, waiting for that slight change in shadow that might herald the blaze of lethal lead that would send him and his friends to their hopefully quick death. Vigilance was most of his task on board this Halifax heavy bomber, and likely his only chance. He moved the controls by rote to peer at the gloom. He heard the crackle of the intercom as his crewmates worked together to deliver their explosive payload on—what was the target again? Oh yeah, Mannheim.

Frankly, it didn't matter what the target was. They all started looking the same—excepting, of course, "the big city," Berlin. That was different. His pulse grew more strident as he flashed back to his most recent trip there and the frustration he felt when his guns jammed as their aircraft was accosted by a fighter.

The memories of that encounter still haunted him. He had seen the enemy aircraft below and off to starboard quarter as it put another Halifax's port outer engine on fire with a quick and accurate burst of gunfire. The bomber went into a dive and disappeared into the overcast, the glow from the flames fading quickly under cover of that thick envelope. Whether the dive was a terminal one or if the crew could extinguish the blaze or bail out, he would likely never learn. The fighter lazily pulled up to bring it dead astern of Len's turret. It was a long shot—600 yards—but it was at the perfect aspect for Len to seek some immediate retribution. As the silhouette clarified into a German single-engine fighter, Len pushed his firing button. A string of lead and tracer rounds erupted from his machine guns, and then as suddenly as they started, his guns stopped less than 100 rounds into his attack. He tried desperately to clear the jam as he saw the fighter roll over to line up another bomber for attack. No doubt alerted to the attacker's presence by either the earlier attack or Len's abortive return fire, the next bomber dove into the clouds just ahead of the long burst emitted by the German. Both aircraft disappeared into the murk of the underlying overcast. Len cursed then as he did again now.

Yes, he had been flying as a last-minute replacement in an unfamiliar air-craft that night, but that was not an excuse to let his brethren down. It would not happen again, he had vowed. The care and effort that he put into the maintenance of his turret would never leave them defenceless again. *This duty will not fail because of me*, he reaffirmed. This was the same silent promise each of the intimately linked crew of seven kept as they rode their Halifax heavy bomber over Nazi Germany. This thought was one of his few comforts as they wended their often long and torturous path to the target. The pilot weaved the plane again.

"Lanc on fire port quarter down!" The voice over the intercom was a comically strained calm but an octave higher than anyone remembered the "sprog" mid-upper gunner possessing. They all knew it was George's first trip on ops and so understood well what the young man must be going through. Len, too, had seen the bomber in trouble but kept it only at the margin of his peripheral vision.

"Don't spoil your rods," came the measured but stern admonishment from the skipper. Robbie was in charge and he didn't brook much point-less chatter from the crew, especially this close to the run-up to the target. Night vision was all that allowed the crew to differentiate the enemy from the neutral background this moonless night provided—key to that, all had learned in one lecture or another, were the differentiated cells on the back of our eyeball. "Cones" told colour while "rods" were photoreceptive. It was easy to forgive George's fascination with the fate of the likely-doomed aircraft below and its seven crew, but his dark-adapted eyes were needed scanning the sky. Something has stricken that bomber and was likely still lurking.

Len redoubled his efforts peering into the void. The turret moved smoothly under his practised hand. This would be his twentieth operation, and since he had arrived at RAF Lissett at the beginning of May in 1943, no fewer than forty-five crews had failed to return. Now here it was, mid-November of the same year. Squadron 158 would put up twenty crews on a good night, and more than double that number were lost in the past six months. It didn't take an Isaac Newton to figure that he was already on borrowed time. Here he was, now flying with his sixth pilot. Most of the previous ones were gone— likely dead. Only faith, fate, or good luck had kept Len from joining them. His friend, Rollie, told him that that was bollocks. He assured him that the one thing all those missing crews lacked on the night they got the chop was Len's sharp eyes in the rear turret. And sometimes he allowed himself that that might be true. But Rollie had failed to return last month—he, too, was probably dead. Maybe it *was* just luck.

The oxygen mask chafed Len's face. Frozen condensation, sweat, and spittle cleaved to his skin and threatened to divide his concentration. Experience and training demanded that he ignore this discomfort. The life-sustaining oxygen that the mask delivered was essential in the rarified atmosphere at this altitude, and any small lapse in his attention could mean their demise.

The aircraft juked sideways once more, and Len felt it intimately. It was almost comforting the way the tail of the Halifax seemed to flick and flip in ways that were unique to this position. Len had been in many other spots in a variety of airplanes throughout his training and operational service, but there was something unique about his backward-gazing perspective opposite to the usual business end of the craft. Of course, to him, this *was* the business end and its movements were, by now, second nature. He smiled to himself as he recalled Robbie telling him how disquieting it was for him to occupy the rear turret in another bomber in which he had hitched a ride. He swore he'd never do it again.

"Navigator, distance to target?" Robbie's cool and clipped query, although not directed at him, reminded Len that his mind should be on the job.

"Five minutes, forty seconds," came the almost immediate reply. The voice, though unfamiliar, was clearly competent—as well it should be. The spare navigator for tonight's operation, Miller, normally flew with one of the Squadron's flight leaders. It was surprising how frequently a "crew" was a collection of spare parts. Pappy, the usual navigator, was on leave, and he was but a replacement for Robbie's original. That said nothing of either man's abilities—after all, Len was relatively new on this crew, too. What you trusted was if a man had made it through operations. They all had, save for George, the clearly wide-eyed man in the mid-upper turret tonight. That intangible quality defined you, but it just may have simply meant that you'd been lucky.

They neared the target. Already there was the occasional burst of flak— well off altitude and track at present. Len continued his survey of the night from the rear turret as he hoped George did up ahead. The air gunners so often seemed separate from the job of the bomber. In the mess and in the pubs, too many times were they teased that they were "just passengers" to have it not sting sometimes. In his heart, Len knew that he was as much a necessary link as the rest.

Len could picture them all now. He knew from experience that the crew were all working on the run-up. Robbie was in charge in the pilot's seat. The aircraft seemed to just be an extension of his lanky body, and he flew with such ease and control that it inspired Len like few others had. Flitting about him, like a worker to a queen bee, was "Lofty," the diminutive flight engineer. He took care of all the needs of both the pilot and bomber because he knew every detail—what was needed and when. Silent now in his "office" was Hale, the wireless operator, and nearby was the navigator's station—tonight manned by the competent replacement. They worked in concert with each other, but now, on the run-up, they could serve best by being quiet. Soon to be very busy was the air bomber, Stan. His view of the target right now must be at once spectacular and daunting, lying as he was in the nose of the aircraft peering through the clear Perspex at the opposite end of the Halifax bomber from Len.

Len checked his watch. The trip seemed to be taking longer than anticipated. In time, the reason became clear. Off to his left he could see a near solid wall of searchlights probing their malevolent fingers into the night. Being found by one usually meant being found by many with the near-inescapable end being shot down by flak or fighters. Robbie had flown around that death trap at the expense of a longer path. *Good show, wot!* Len didn't care one whit if it meant cold tea on a tardy but safe return.

"Bombing on green T.I.s, Skipper," was Stan's sure call from the nose. Briefing warned of dummy target indicators being lit by the enemy. Although the Germans tried to replicate the Pathfinder Force's target marking, they could never quite get the colours right to the trained eye.

"I only see green and yellow, Stan, and the greens are cascading." replied Robbie. That the green flares were seen to be dropping from the sky usually ensured that they were genuine. Pilot and air bomber were on the same page. It was going to be a good prang. Len felt the extra drag that the open bomb doors created on their flight. He redoubled his scan of the darkness, because he knew that Robbie must stop his diversionary weaving and now fly straight and level to bomb release.

"Steady … Steady… Left … Steady …" came Stan's monotone directions to Robbie. Robbie's track was usually so good that it took very little correction. There was the usual pause and then the call of "Bombs gone!" The relieved aircraft almost seemed to sigh with the lightening of the load.

This was the part Len hated most, the interminable wait for the photoflash of the target so the SqIntO back at base would have something to do once the bomb photos were developed. Len was not certain what the Intelligence Section ever gleaned from those blurry, streaky photos. He could get the same effect by pointing an open camera at a wiener-roast back home. But those were the orders, so they did it. His peripheral vision caught several flashes below; one must have been theirs, because he felt the aerodynamically smoother flight that a closed bomb-bay ensured.

They had bombed from the north, so their briefed return path took them several miles south of the target before they would turn back home. Robbie's earlier dodge of the searchlights south of Frankfurt took them farther east than planned, but not so far that they might be a straggler. Suddenly the great bomber lurched as if to avoid a collision. Len half expected to see the dark shape of another RAF heavy bomber moving past as had happened before. Putting several hundred aircraft over a single target was not without consequence. Instead what happened was even more frightening. Searchlight!

Night turned day in a fraction of a second in Len's cramped turret. He instinctively closed his eyes, but the brilliant, bluish light seared through his eyelids. After hours of carefully accustomed night vision, the brightness stung. He squinted his eyes open to see his turret in detail that the English sun had never revealed. Reflex took hold as he drew his head down lower into his flying suit. The Halifax lurched violently as Robbie threw it into well practised combat manoeuvres. A banked dive to port through hundreds of feet, a sharp climb through a similar altitude, then turn to starboard through the climb, then repeat in the opposite direction—the aptly named "corkscrew." Len had a better name for it right about now; he'd call it "Hell." The changes in speed and altitude were designed to throw off enemy fighters and now, hopefully, a searchlight. But it was not working. One after another, more searchlights snapped onto the master beam, and it grew impossibly brighter in the aircraft. They were "coned."

Most of the boys had seen other bombers coned. It was impressive as the multiple searchlights intersected on their prey like the silk in a web. But Len had seen every case end with a bomber on fire from a fighter attack or a cascade of arcing embers from a direct flak hit. Little to choose between the two, but at least with a fighter, you might have a chance in combat. There was nothing to do but try to hang on and strain to see if he could see the end coming.

Len was jostled in his swaddling turret. There was scarcely room to move within it in level flight, but the wild gyrations the skipper was putting the Halifax through were always made worse in the extreme tail end that was his domain. Still, the buffeting was reduced by the size of the enclosure and his carefully cinched lap belt. Len's thoughts went to Stan, who likely thought most of his job was finished after letting go the bombs but who was now likely being bashed around the more cavernous nose of the aircraft like a kernel in a thresher. Stan was a great chap and would likely spin a good yarn to tell about it over a pint or two when they got home. If they got home.

Through the blinding glare of the searchlights, Len thought he saw something gaining on them. It seemed just a shape, but there was no question what it could be. The fighter was dead astern and too far for the Halifax's quad .303 Browning machine guns to reach. While he was directly behind, the bomber's best chance was to continue to corkscrew. Len waited for any deviation in the fighter's path or for him to close to his gun's effective range. The fighter followed their wild gyrations as if attached by a tow cable. It could be discerned now, a single engine fighter—an Me109. Its pilot must be licking his lips with such an easy, illuminated prey.

The fighter slipped slightly to the starboard beam, and Len saw their chance. He gave the one order that a gunner can issue and have it followed forthwith. "Starboard. Go!" His hoarse voice filled their intercom headsets, and Robbie immediately changed the direction of his corkscrew. At almost the same instant, the fighter opened fire with cannon and machine guns. Len observed tracer rounds seemingly weaving past the left side of the aircraft, aimed at where the aircraft had been just a second ago. He felt and saw sparks where shells ripped through the port tail structures.

The sudden change in flight attitude seemed to surprise the fighter pilot, and he now came into Len's gun sight. He was at maximum range, and you normally would not open fire on an enemy so far away so as to not reveal your position with your tracer shells. But there was no chance of stealth now—with a dozen searchlights on them, anyone within fifteen miles could see them! "Try this, you Jerry bastard," Len spoke to no-one as he pressed his fire button for a near zero deflection long burst from his machine guns.

The fighter broke suddenly midway through the return fire. Len felt he must have hit him but could see no fire or smoke. The deterrence seemed to have worked, for the enemy aircraft was soon lost from sight. With the combat, Robbie's evasion seemed to become even more violent. Either Len's eyes were becoming adapted to the light, or some of the searchlights seemed to lose their prey. No—incrementally, the intensity of the light in which they were bathed diminished until one last swerve to port seemed to leave only the bluish light of the master searchlight on them. Then as suddenly as it started, they were in total darkness again. Len could make out the programmed probing weave of the columns of light now behind them. They were free.

The skipper gradually reduced his corkscrew to a waggle as he called for his crew to report in. One by one, as they gathered their wits, each reported that they were in one piece. Reports of damage and a quick survey by the crew revealed that they had taken several hits, but they were not ablaze, nor did they seem to be leaking any critical fluids. Robbie reminded the gunners that fighters were likely still out there and to keep a sharp eye out. Len needed no such warning, but he chuckled to himself that George, the first-timer in the mid-upper turret could not have had a better demonstration as to why he should remain vigilant. *He'll likely survive a tour because of it*, he thought.

Through the ordeal, Len had fired all of the 400 odd rounds offered in defense of the bomber. He had done his job in protecting his crew—his friends, his brothers. Len's thoughts turned briefly to his family back in Canada. He was close to his siblings, but there was a bond that seemed even stronger with these boys on this still-droning heavy bomber, and he felt closer to them now than ever.

He would likely never be able to explain the camaraderie to anyone who had not experienced it. There was always pride in a job well done … even more so when it felt you were one of the very few striking back against the tyranny that the Nazis and their cronies were now proving to be. Yes, the Axis had capitulated in Africa, and the Allies were now fighting on the ground in Italy. But Hitler's "Fortress Europe" was still largely unmolested by anything save Bomber Command. For years now, it seemed they alone were left to carry the fight to Germany. And the battle had been well and truly joined by this branch. Len had always been made to feel a part of any crew with whom he flew, but tonight, he thought, it finally felt complete. The events of the night, the adrenaline pumping, the decisive actions, and the satisfaction of the "D.C.O."—Duty Carried Out, he would write in his logbook later had him feeling like a keenly honed blade. He scanned the skies with a renewed confidence in this crew and in himself.

"Wizard work, all of you," said Robbie as they neared the North Sea coast of Yorkshire. "Especially you gunners." The rest of the crew broke protocol and chimed in on the intercom to congratulate the gunners. Some was understandable deflection of praise by all who had done admirably this night, but Len allowed some to cascade over his broad shoulders. The dimly lit familiar shape of Flamborough Head, that certain harbinger of home, passed to his left as they surely lost altitude in the still, pre-dawn murk. Tonight, he felt "operational." Tonight, he had earned his wings.

2

My father watched patiently as I tried to tie my shoes by our back door. He had asked if I wanted to come with him and go to our meat locker to pick up a roast Mom would cook on Sunday. Being asked to go for a car ride was as rare as having roast, so I knew I could not squander this opportunity. It would only be us, so I would be certain to be in the front seat! I tried desperately to make my five-year-old fingers emulate the bow-tying that Mother had painstakingly demonstrated, but the best I could manage was either loose loops or something I knew would end in an irrevocable "granny knot." I had practised, but the arcane twists and turns of her hands never quite made sense to me. I was on the verge of tears.

"Here, Son ..." he said in his quiet way. Being called "Son" was always soothing—if he took the time to recall your given name, you knew you might be in trouble. He slipped the still-untied shoes from my feet and started to completely unlace them. "I will show you how I do mine."

His thick fingers took out the criss-crossed laces that seemed to be standard in all my siblings' shoes in the boot-tray at the side entrance to the house. He then started to lace them, one eyelet across to the one opposite so that they crossed underneath and there were only transverse parallel lines of laces across the top. It seemed more complicated, but precise and elegant. I recognized the pattern from his shoes.

"Daddy... why do the laces go that way?" I knew that there must be a reason for this rather elaborate procedure.

"If you ditch your airplane in the water, you can just slip a knife into the laces and cut them all and get out of your shoes quickly to swim," he said simply, pantomiming the action you would take with a blade in your hand. I accepted this silently. It was only many years later that I considered how unlikely this event truly was, given that we lived in the middle of the Canadian Prairies, thousands of miles from any significant water body, and that our family was far too financially strapped to fly anywhere, in any case.

He then hunched behind me and bade me to slip on my shoe as he reached on either side of each foot in turn and tied them for me in a way that seemed neat and simple. It looked like it could be a "granny knot," but it carried two loops outside the square of the knot. The loops of the bow hung smartly on either side of the shoe. This made sense and seemed appropriately precise to festoon the new pattern of laces.

"See?" he explained, pulling one loose end. "It is still tied even if one end gets pulled." I confirmed that this was so. He then pulled the other loose end, and the simple overhand knot that started all shoe-tying was all that was left. "Now you try."

I did as he had and came up with something vaguely similar but ultimately too loose to be of any real good. He showed me again and after only a few more of my attempts, the result was good enough for us to be on our way. I sprinted with pride to the car and flung open the hefty door of the old green Mercury Meteor, taking the treasured position normally occupied by Mom. Dad was several moments behind me.

I sat looking at my shoes, admiring the elegant precision of the laces while running over the procedure in my mind. I would never need to be shown again, and with some smugness, I noted that none of my five siblings did their shoes this way. As Dad put the car in gear to drive, I looked up at him while pointing at my feet. "Where did you learn that, Daddy?"

He seemed to take a moment. "In training," he said finally with no further elaboration. I craned to peek out the passenger window as we drove.

Len flung his RCAF service cap down on his bunk. How many times was he going to be told that he wasn't old enough, smart enough, skilled enough … *good* enough! Why did he even join up if they were just going to tell him that? He had heard enough of that at home. His anger raced even with his disappointment as he stared out the barracks window, hands thrust deep in his uniform pockets. He took a deep, calming breath. His pulse was still pounding in his ears as he surveyed the burgeoning late spring scene outside. The earth seemed hopeful, but he was far from feeling the same.

The sea of red ink it took to grade his last examination still burned in his mind's eye. He knew before it was even submitted that that would be the result. He had prayed that some miracle would render his more fervent guesses to be correct. But he knew in his heart that what the Lord had envisioned in his future was yet to be revealed to him here. Perhaps He was waiting for a more critical time to answer Len's prayers—he knew it wasn't going to be on that mathematical exam.

Len thought he had done well so far. At the Manning Depot in Brandon, after enlistment, he had learned to be a soldier. He had drilled and studied. He had also worked harder than at any harvest. He was also in far better shape than shovelling grain or throwing bales could ever render. At home, he had worked very much on his own—doing the chores no-one else would. That was service to the family. It had taught him the importance of duty, but it was the air force that taught him to work in a team. Every lesson he took to heart. Every detail was important because the team depended on him. Nothing was too small to overlook, and his keenness for this concept had been duly noted. He had hoped it would be enough to carry him through, but the clucking and obvious consternation of his instructors intimated otherwise.

Already this was his second chance. Len's superiors had held him back from his previous class here at ITS (Initial Training School) in a fair chance to permit him to catch up. He had apparently shown enough promise to have earned that, but he now knew the latitude that had been extended to him had now been exceeded.

So he would not be a pilot. *There it was.* The first step was in admitting and accepting it. But he knew that he was capable of more than the many others he had seen opt for less challenging service along the way. There is no doubt that he envied those few that seemed born to be pilots, but circumstances just did not favour him. He silently cursed his inadequate education. He cursed the timing of the war. Couldn't it have waited until he was finished high school? He cursed his own inability to catch up with the others who had had a head start.

Damn it. Damn it all to hell!

"What's the good word?" Len started slightly as Nick's cheery query preceded him as he strode into the room. Nick, at 5' 10", was likely three inches taller than Len and as slender as a rail. With his straight blond hair, he could not have been more different from his stocky and powerfully-built roommate. He was a good man, and he and Len were fast friends despite growing up over a thousand miles from one another. They had shared many a triumph and failure since they met here. It seemed that Len had been in training too long for this to be *Initial* Training School. At least being in Toronto's No.1 ITS offered a variety of diversions on evenings and weekends. But the stultifying classroom work and barely scraping through academically was wearing pretty thin.

"There *are* no good words." Len's reply was soft as he continued to stare out the window. He turned to face Nick's slowly disappearing grin. "I enlisted nearly eight months ago, and I seem to be getting further and further away from *anything!*" He punctuated this with a chop at the air with his hand. "I pounded the square for three months in Brandon, stooged around in St. Thomas for six weeks before they finally got their finger out and sent me here, and now I am probably farther from flying than I've ever been!"

Nick shook his head in resigned commiseration. He too knew of the frequent disappointments they had shared since they met here in late March 1942. It sometimes seemed the war would be over before they ever got into the fray. "At least you have never crashed the Link Trainer!" Len couldn't help but join Nick's laughter at the recall of that afternoon. Nick's dishevelled comportment as he exited the ground-based training apparatus and the apoplectic berating by the instructor was right out of a movie.

But Nick never knew the embarrassment of the academic failures that Len endured. They were not as public but just as damning. If the truth be told, Len had not even finished Grade 11, yet here he was being tested on algebra, trigonometry, and other arcane subjects that seemed to have little to do with flying an airplane. What was it all for? His own performance in the Link was passable, but in the classroom, it was becoming increasingly obvious that he was not going to cut it. Even with Nick's extra help—and it seemed to come easily to Nick—he just could not wrap his head around all those number problems.

"Let's find a beer," Nick offered and then quickly added, "You buy." Len chuckled as he retrieved his wedge cap and secured it at its usual rakish angle on his thick wavy nap. Despite them being told that the white flash of "aircrew in training" in their cap would lead to women swooning as they passed, they had yet to really encounter it. The birds all seemed to go for the officers. Maybe the downside of being in "Hogtown" was that there was just too much competition. He seemed to get a lot more attention from the prairie girls back in Regina as a simple recruit. In uniform back home in Lampman, he was a god!

"You know what the regulars tell the skirts?" Nick remarked as they passed yet another woman who pointedly avoided their hopeful glances. "They tell them the medical officer makes us wear the white in the cap while we've got 'the clap' and are still infectious!" he continued, laughing.

Len felt his eyes widen as he looked at the offending cap on Nick's head, and he briefly considered whipping his own from his head. The chit that accompanied being "out of uniform" seemed a toss-up when weighing it against the adverse effect it seemed to have on any potential female company. The choice was made more difficult with his performance on the last exercise in navigation class.

"Jealous buggers," was all Len could say in resignation. He seemed defeated at every turn.

The two naturally fell in step as they walked to their favourite pub on Eglington Avenue. There were many people on the street on this fine June late afternoon. Len had almost gotten used to the rush and bustle of the big city. Everyone seemed to be going somewhere. Life at home in Saskatchewan had been so much different. He had thought that the streets of Regina had been busy compared to the easy, glacial pace of his hometown, but this was an entirely altered state. He was unsure if it was that every face was unfamiliar or if it was their reluctance to look him in the eye. At home, he was just "the younger brother," and everyone there knew that. Here, it seemed they could tell something that even he didn't know. It was disquieting. He offered Nick a cigarette, and it was quickly taken and lit.

The only clue that there was a war on was the preponderance of men in uniform. Most were trainees like themselves, but the prospect of encountering someone requiring tribute had them careful to secret their smokes in their left hands lest they be in jankers for the dreaded "smoking salute." Neither of them could afford that breach. Not at this stage of training.

The pub was not yet too crowded so the draughts were as easy to obtain as the table in the corner. As promised, Len had bought the first round, and the first sip of cool ale tasted sweet. Len sighed and leaned back. Nick regarded him and said at some length, "What's gotten into you today? Has 'Chunky' lit into you again? You shouldn't pay him never-mind! You know he's only ever flown a desk."

"Chunky" was the name whispered as epithet for the rather rotund navigation instructor at ITS. Pilot Officer Burns could pass as a reasonable facsimile of a barrage balloon as he floated about the front of the classroom. There was much speculation as to how he had earned that rank if he could never fit in a cockpit, let alone through an aircraft hatch. But he could certainly determine your fate at the school, so any untoward comments by the trainees were uttered far from earshot.

Len's eyes barely flickered from considering the disappearing head on the draught in front of him. "I don't think I can hack it anymore." He glanced up meaningfully at Nick. This is the closest he had come to giving up on the dream of being a pilot. He wanted so desperately to get out from his older brothers' shadows. Their birthright was the family farm. Yes, he had a younger brother, but he was still the "baby" and too young to handle all the menial tasks that were his at home. Dad was dead, along with another brother—dead in an embarrassing tragedy that he didn't even want to think about. There was no place for him at home in Saskatchewan, and now there seemed to be no place for him here.

Nick seemed to take a long time to respond. He seemed to know that Len was beyond the usual remedy of a couple of pints and a bucking-up. "What are you going to do?"

"I am going to ask for AG," Len said as he looked up for a reaction. Nick obliged by raising his thin eyebrows, shaking his head slightly, and emitting a low whistle.

"A pilot is just a driver. It's the air gunner who gets to shoot Krauts." Len continued, "My eyes are perfect, and my trigger finger works just fine." He grabbed his glass suddenly and took a long swig. "And I won't need any goddamn algebra to shoot the buggers between the eyes," he said quickly, slamming the near-empty glass down.

"I had a feeling you were going to say something like that," Nick replied before taking his own matching draught. "I have been thinking much the same, 'cept I won't be joining you as 'arse-end Charlie!' My eyes are fine with the eye chart but nowhere else. And I think my fizzers have pissed off too many of the muckety-mucks to ever be recommended for flight school." Nick paused and finally added, "What do you think of me as your navigator?"

"Navigator?" Len teasingly exclaimed. "Didn't you need directions to Yonge Street last weekend? You couldn't find your ass with both hands!" They both laughed and Nick retorted, "Gunner? Who couldn't aim to hit the pisser the same night!"

Len hoisted his glass and bade Nick to do the same. "Well, we had had a few of these. Cheers … and may all your plots be true!"

Nick replied as he held his glass high and winked, "And may all your targets be blonde!" Their nearly-drained glasses met with a sharp report and they summarily downed what was left; their choices now sealed even if their orders were not officially cut.

As Nick left the table to get the next round, Len considered his decision. He *had* come a long way. When he stood with his cousins outside his aunt's boarding house in Regina, resplendent in their new RCAF recruit blues, they had all sworn to replicate that photo with their double-winged pilot badges proudly displayed. Now Richie had already re-mustered as an AG, and Jim had taken a tradesman job. Len held on to the dream longer than the others, but it was certainly time to face the inevitable and make a choice while the choice was still ostensibly his to make. He had still made it farther than he had heard whispered he would. He would not be alone in carrying his surname into the war, but he'd be the only one of his siblings to do so. There was no small amount of satisfaction in that.

Tomorrow Len would talk to "Chunky" or "Butch" or "Wheezer" or any of the other men who held their fate in their hands but who were far better known by their unkind monikers. Maybe he was not pilot material, but he certainly was fit for aircrew, and he intended to show all of those who had suggested otherwise that he could carry his load and the fight to Jerry. "Tail end Charlie" he might be, but there would be no doubting his resolve or his dedication.

Nick returned with a couple more draughts. "Drink up, my boy, for tomorrow we die." Nick was always one for gallows humour. Len hoisted his glass and countered, "Or at least this evening we march!" He had not forgotten that they still had evening parade. They had better not linger. Len still had buttons to shine and shoes to polish.

3

The roiling cloud mass loomed ominously as the rolling peals of thunder signalled the impending storm. Prairie thunderstorms are a sight to behold because so little impedes the view of them—trees and hills are, of course, foreign here. In our yard, Dad was pointing out some of the swirling while trying to connote the violence of the movements with several quick opposing hand gestures. My older sister and I listened with our rapt attention evenly divided between his explanation and the threatening atmosphere. The first few spits of rain came with a sudden cooling breeze and he shepherded us under the eaves of our small house where we would continue our more restricted but still careful observations.

Dad loved thunderstorms. But he seemed to know so much about all the clouds. He spoke of them like they were old friends—the "mackerel skies" that were rows of tiny, scale-like puffs of high white cloud that he claimed foretold of pleasant weather, or the towering turrets of what is known as castellanus. He called those "hail clouds." I never knew if his knowledge came from years of careful observation on the farm where he grew up, or from his experience flying through them. Whatever it was, his tone always suggested intimate acquaintance.

A flash of lightning caught all our attention. I am certain my widened eyes were not unnoticed by my father, but he just calmly started counting slowly and quietly as he fixed me with a softly reassuring gaze. If he was not going to be frightened, I surely would not be. He reached a count of thirteen before he was interrupted by a tumult of echoing thunder.

"About two and a half miles away," he said matter-of-factly. I was only happy that the count had not exceeded my limited math skills. Grade 1 had only taken me so far! I did not yet understand what relation the counting had to how far away the storm was.

Almost coincident with the subsidence of the peal of thunder came yet another familiar sound—Mom poked her head out of the side door and trilled, "Len! Get in the house!" She so worried about him. Only later did I understand why she seemed so protective—and how frail he really was. I knew she cared about my sister and I outside with him, but her first thought was of him.

"If there's one up there with my name on it, it's gonna get me anyway!" he growled in response. Mom clucked and fidgeted with no small exasperation, but with resignation, retreated into the relative safety of the house. Dad's words seemed to hang in the air as we hunched closer together and to the wall from the building downpour.

This waiting was the worst part.

Len had been on squadron for nearly five months, and during that time more than twice as many operations were scheduled than had gone ahead. The vagaries of the daily weather in East Yorkshire were quite extreme, let alone the uncertainty of forecasts for the projected path over the continent and especially for the target. At one time it bothered him that so much energy was wasted in gearing up for these SNAFUs. These days, it more irked him that it all just seemed to be postponing the inevitable. He was certain that some measure of that ambivalence was shared by most of his colleagues.

It seemed so different from the early days after his arrival in England. Getting used to the weather—the long, cold, dreary winter of 1942–43. Getting crewed up with Barry and all that flying in Scotland and Yorkshire— the thrill of getting above the damp murk of the English weather nearly every day—was only eight months ago. The closeness of those comrades he grew to know better than his brothers seemed like yesterday, and yet it seemed to be in a different lifetime. This was his life now, spent waiting for who knows what. It gave a lot of time for contemplation … probably too much.

Len leaned against the briefing building, enjoying the comfort of a long drag on his cigarette. It was a pleasant early September afternoon. Yes, it was windy, but mainly clear. The southwest winds, experience told him, suggested a good night for operations. Surely there would be no cancelation tonight, but he had been wrong before. All it takes is one of those boffins in the Meteorological Section to see the wrong thing in his crystal ball and the whole thing could be scrubbed.

Met boys, Len thought to himself as he took another draw on his Players and inhaled deeply. They always got the raspberries whenever they took the briefing stage. They may as well be wearing turbans and addressed as "Swami" for the quality of predictions they made. He could tell better from his casual glance at the clouds and the windsock what the next twenty-four hours would bring. They ought to just concentrate on getting it right for the target. The sooner they could prang Jerry into submission, the sooner they could all go home.

Home.

He hadn't let himself think of that in months. It seemed the more time he had to think of such things, the further he pushed it from his consciousness. Home took more of his attention during his time at OTU. Operational Training was always busy-busy-busy with flying nearly every day, but he never lost sight of home because there always seemed to be a next day. And at the end of all those next days, there would finally be home again. But here, on an operational Squadron, tomorrow didn't really exist. If you were smart and didn't think about tomorrow, you might get through today. He pushed home and tomorrow to the back corners of his mind.

Len saw Ernie approaching, no doubt coming back from his required navigation briefing that always preceded the general briefing. He had the jaunty step of a man who knew his future—at least as far as the next twelve hours could take him. Ernie was another Canadian at Lissett and a nice guy—despite being from Ontario and having a commission. Len dismissed this cynicism quickly from his thoughts; there was no place for it here. Besides, maybe Ernie had some real gen.

"You still coming with us tonight, Len?" Ernie said with a fractional toss of his head. Len knew better than to look for clues about the target that would have been conveyed to the pilots, navigators, and air bombers at their separate meetings. If he had asked, he probably would have been told, but not asking made it much easier for Ernie to keep the security. Truth be told, the name of the target didn't matter too much when there was a push on.

"'Sposed to," Len said as he tossed down his cigarette and squashed its smolder into the damp earth with the toe of his boot. "Freddie's not going to be back, and Roy already gave me the word." Fred was the rear turret gunner on Ernie's crew, and Roy was the captain of the kite. Fred had nipped off to marry his girlfriend. He had tried to schedule his wedding during the waxing moon when Bomber Command usually eased off operations, but the boys at High Wycombe seemed to be on a quota this month, so the forty-eight-hour leave granted for his nuptials was in the middle of a drive.

Len was a "spare bod" on squadron and ever since his original crew was dispersed, he was a frequent replacement on other crews because of absences, both planned and otherwise. Those picking him said that it was because he was a wizard gunner and mate. Len suspected it was because he was lucky enough to make it through half a tour. Either way, it felt better to be a pal than a pariah.

"Freddie sure was browned off that we couldn't make it to the do." Ernie continued pulling out his own pack of Sweet Caps and offered Len one of the cigarettes; he declined, politely holding up his hand. "But he seemed chuffed to be tying the knot just the same. We'll put it all right when he is done converting his 'target for tonight' into the 'trouble and strife.'"

They both laughed deeply. Len had not yet flown with Ernie's bunch, but knew them as one of the many closely-knit crews that had made it through their first few operations and were therefore safer to get to know. The propensity for sprog crews to disappear in their first five odd sorties meant that they were often left alone until they proved they might stick around. It had the ancillary effect of making a crew bond even more tightly. But that hurdle had been overcome with this crew, and Len had warmed up to them considerably.

Of course, experience was no guarantee of a crew's survival. It was just last month that the wingco, the Squadron Commander, had failed to return from operations. That should have put paid to notion that only new crews were subject to loss. But tradition was a hard nut to crack—especially in the RAF.

They both tried to lessen the subsequent lingering silence by scanning the sky and assessing the weather. Though their consensus was unspoken, they both knew they'd be flying tonight.

"Wanna go in?" Ernie said finally. "The others will be by in a jiffy. Briefing will be starting soon." Len turned and followed his compatriot into the building.

The air was already hazy blue from the accumulated cigarette smoke, despite the briefing room being only about half full. The unintelligible murmur of dozens of conversations was comforting but still managed to heighten the anxiety that always preceded operations. A quick scan revealed that no one else from their crew had yet arrived, so Ernie picked some empty seats near the middle of the room that would accommodate all seven.

As the room began to fill several minutes before the scheduled starting time, Len noticed the airmen's spatial distribution. Where people ended up was an interesting study. There were the nervous new crews up front. They were easy to spot with their almost nonchalant anxiety. They were interspersed with some of the old heads on squadron who had always taken a place up front and knew better than to change the luck that had brought them this far. There were the others whom had accepted that where they sat mattered very little to their fortune, for they had been around long enough to see those of a variety of experience get the chop. And there were those who preferred to loiter at the back and at the sides—their nervous energy more easily assuaged by remaining standing.

The rest of the crew sauntered in just before the Squadron Commander was due. Ernie's beckoning wave brought them smartly over and greetings were exchanged. Len knew most of them at least well enough to talk to. He knew he was the outsider, but he wanted to show that he could fit in with the team seamlessly. No, he was not Freddie, but he wanted them to know that their vital trust was reciprocal.

Roy was immersed in an animated discussion with Ketch, the crew's flight engineer, about some problem with their aircraft. Their Halifax Mark II was unit "F" on the squadron and they had flown it exclusively. They knew it as *F for Freddie*, even though the RAF had now changed their phonetic alphabet— "F" was now "Fox." That may well be, but with a "Freddie" on the crew, Roy and the boys would not know their kite by any other name. From what Len could glean from the conversation, the problem with the oxygen system had been rectified by the ground crew. He knew that the crew had not completed their operation last night and had returned early. He now understood what had happened, and he was relieved to hear that the ship was now in good order. It seemed the rest of the crew was equally pleased. This Halibag had been good to them!

There was an unseen call to attention as the station brass strode in, and it was acknowledged with reasonable alacrity. The new wingco took advantage of the near silence to put the boys at ease, "Sit down, gentlemen. Smoke them if you've got them." This despite the near opaque pall of smoke that already hung thickly in the air. "The target for tonight is Munich." There were scattered grumbles from those few who had not already heard or guessed the destination. Len had suspected from the early timing today that they would be flying some distance. The over nine hours round trip to Bavaria would be as much a test of his bladder as of his abilities. So long in the air made them an inviting target for flak or fighters. He would need to be alert.

The briefing dragged on through Len's mental preparations, and he scarcely paid attention to what was being said. As an air gunner, especially in the rear turret, he already knew what he needed to know: "when" and "how far." Indeed, he was part of the team, and he knew the enormity of that responsibility, but the details of the operation were largely immaterial. He was there for his eyes and his alertness. He lit another cigarette and tried to relax. Now they were into the meteorological briefing. There was still a chance of adverse weather over the target, but the Met Section thought it was even odds that they would be on. Whether they went ahead tonight as scheduled or were scrubbed, it was going to be a long night.

Squadron 158 was to attack in two of the six waves planned—second and fifth. Roy's crew, in which Len was now an accepted member, at least for tonight, was to be in the former, so they needed to have wheels up by shortly after 1900 hours to make the plan work. There were things to be said to be either early or late in the attack. Len preferred being early to keep what element of surprise could be gained, even after such a lengthy flight. Some preferred to be in the later waves of attack, hoping that the defending fighters would be on the ground for refuelling by the time they arrived. But mitigating this was that if the attack was successful, and the fires that they had hopefully started underlit the forecast low clouds, the silhouettes of the higher-flying bombers would make them easy pickings for the fighters.

It really didn't matter. These issues had been bandied *ad nauseam* in messes, pubs, and in one's own mind since Bomber Command was formed. Nearly everyone in the room knew, to a man, that if they did their job perfectly, they still might not come back. This was luck, and this was operational flying in a war. Every man in the room also believed that they would do their job and it would be someone else who didn't make it back. It was the only way that you could climb into that lumbering, draughty beast night after night.

The wingco wrapped up the briefing with a confident urge for a good show. It was not the shrill boosterism of the type who knows he's sending people to try an impossible task, but instead a rather avuncular pat on the back. It didn't seem at all unusual that the man was likely, at most, no more than a year or two older than the men he was discharging to do their duty.

The room dissolved into a cacophony of conversations. Al, the other air gunner on the crew, muttered to no-one in particular, "Freddie picked a perfect day to get hitched." He then acknowledged Len and said cheerfully, "Fancy a little trip to München tonight?"

Len took a second to process the use of the German language name for the target but tried to suppress any puzzlement. Al, from his appearance, had a good ten years on Len and was clearly far more erudite.

"Oh yeah," he replied with a shrug. "Always looking for a new sticker on my trunk."

Al laughed in appreciation of the casual, quick response. He gave Len a playful jab and a wink. "Good show. We'll try to not keep you awake."

The aircrew filed out into the early September evening. There was enough time for the crew to partake of the traditional operational snack, a luxury afforded to the aircrew: fried eggs on toast. It helped fill the nervous time before the intensity of an operational flight, but the novelty had long worn off for Len. His cadre for tonight, however, seemed quite keen, so he fell in lockstep with them. The somersaults his stomach was performing might be slightly sedated by the solid if somewhat greasy bulk the mess would turn out. He listened to the idle chatter of the crew as they walked while he scanned the skies once more. He hoped the pleasant weather would hold for a few more weeks. His long-awaited two-week leave was starting in a couple of days. This was likely his last sortie for a while.

With the practised informality of the traditional meal behind them, there was little to do but lounge around the crew quarters until it was time to make their way to their bomber. With the nice weather, many found a dry spot in the surrounding grass outside. Some crews quickly got a game of pontoon going, for it always helped pass the time. Len stayed with his crew outside as most lit up yet another cigarette. He was in no hurry to get kitted up—sitting too long in full gear, especially as a gunner, was something Len had learned to avoid. But he hoped they would not linger too long, for he had never flown in *F for Freddie* before and was uncertain how a different ground crew would have left his turret, or indeed, how diligent the man he was replacing had been with the equipment. He tried to balance his anxiousness with the necessity to fit in with the routine of this unfamiliar crew.

Talk turned naturally to Freddie, the absent gunner and eager groom. Len could have been offended by the attention afforded the man for whom he was now standing in, but he knew well the dynamics of an aircrew. It was difficult to forget what with Squadron 158's motto found liberally plastered about the station: "Strength in Unity." Their thoughts in this idle time would be naturally with their absent friend.

"I wonder where Freddie's taken 'er t'night," mused Ketch. "I don't suppose 'is forty-eight hours would let 'em get too far 'way. I 'ope he gets a bit o' peace 'n quiet for 'is conjugal duties. She's a right fine lass, she is."

There were general sounds of agreement from those gathered, but Len could offer nothing, having never seen the lady in question or her photo. He simply could not fathom making such a commitment in these circumstances. Perhaps Freddie felt that the vows would protect him. Maybe he felt she was luckier than a rabbit's foot. Or maybe there was no reason to it at all. He had seen many people make inexplicable choices, and others might feel the same about his.

"He could have done much worse!" Roy finally said. "You hear that 'Death-Kiss' Peggy lost another one last week on the trip to the 'big city'"? Peggy was a station WAAF who had the remarkable proclivity to get romantically attached to some poor airman just to have him "go for a Burton." The latest, who failed to return on operations to Berlin, was the third one so far. It was only the blind bravado of aircrew that steadfastly believed that it would always be "the other guy" that kept her dance card full. It was either that or the unflagging drive of hormones in this company of young men.

"The air force oughta send that fucking tart to Hamburg!" spat Simm, the usually taciturn air bomber.

The vehemence of that pronouncement served to stifle the conversation. Len looked at his watch in the hope that this might signal his readiness to get out to the aircraft, but the others still seemed to be studying the grass. He was about to say something to underline his concern when the sight of an unexpected figure walking briskly toward them made him pause. Ketch lifted his head and bolted upright.

"Cor love a duck—would you look at that!" Everyone's eyes widened at Ketch's exclamation, but all were positively dumbstruck when they looked to see Freddie striding toward them with a grin as wide as all outdoors. To a man the crew surrounded their returning gunner, emitting hoots and laughs while alternately slapping the man's shoulders or pumping his hand enthusiastically. Len stood awkwardly to one side, certain that he should not intrude.

"What the hell are you doing here, man?" Roy interjected. "We weren't expecting a royal send-off."

"I just talked to Flight, Skipper, and 'e sez I can come with you if you want. I talked it over with the missus, and she agrees that it'd be better to fly with my mates now than to 'ave to do a make-up flight with some sprog crew down 'd road." Freddie gave a wink. "'Sides, we're due for our stand down this month and that will give more time 't get away with the little woman."

Len could not argue with this logic. As much as he felt that Roy's crew would have been satisfied to fly with him in the rear turret, he would not be offended if the crew wanted to remain whole. They had made it this far intact, why change the luck? If Freddie did not fly with them tonight, he might be required to complete his tour with another crew, and that was always a crapshoot. Len knew that uncertainty all too well. He unconsciously took a step back.

Roy looked wordlessly at his now superfluous air gunner, but Len just nodded and started to undo the few items he had already donned. He felt awkward now amongst this crew—suddenly an outsider. He turned to walk slowly back into the crew room but could still hear the animated conversation behind him.

"Where did you leave her?" Ernie asked.

"I din't," Freddie said excitedly. "I brought 'er back to watch us off. I told 'er to head up that road 'cause the wind is from the southwest ..."

The conversation faded as Len entered the crew room past the last stages of the other crews' card games. They took little notice of him as he put his kit away in silence. Len was glad he was not flying eight or nine hours tonight under a nearly quarter moon, but he was disappointed at not stroking another operation off his tour. At least the early start tonight meant that there was still time to catch a bus into Bridlington. He was sure he could find a few mates at the Brunswick or some other watering hole. He had one full day left before his leave, and he was almost certain there'd be no more ops before then. He walked briskly to where he had left his bicycle.

Several hours later found Len alighting from the transport that had deposited him at the entrance of his appointed communal area. The walk to his quarters in the cool, quiet autumn air took away some of the glow that had been engendered by the pints he had knocked back. He smiled at the memory of the knot of well-dressed civilians that the transport had passed on the Burton Agnes Road on their way into Brid—certainly the lady in the spiffy dress and gloves was the new bride. She was conspicuous as she stood staring with her back to the wind, waiting to wish her new groom well. Len also wished them the very best.

Weariness overtook Len as he entered his quarters. It had been yet another long day of anticipation and anxiety that now just seemed wasted. When he fell into his bunk in the nearly deserted hut, he wondered how much sleep he could get before the exhausted occupants of the other beds would fill them after tonight's long sortie. Sotted sleep quickly quelled his empathetic thoughts.

Morning brought news that the only crew from which there was no word was Roy's. Time had long since passed that they might have ended up at another base, so they were now posted as FTR—Failed to Return. It was not the first time that Len had felt the strange detachment of knowing that men he had just talked to were now likely dead. But he was still in awe of the caprice that had him still standing here. The one with his name on it had not yet found him.

4

I could never sleep in the car. Even though it was dark on this late August evening as the waning moon cast an ethereal light on the prairie landscape and my siblings had all succumbed to the highway's whine, I was wide awake. Four of us shared the back seat of Dad's Mercury Meteor— my brother to my left behind Dad, and two of my sisters to my right, behind Mom. My younger sister, four years my junior, was silently lying with her head in mother's lap. While Morpheus had long since taken my siblings into his somniferous arms, I sat bolt upright.

It had been a long day of visiting my father's family in the Lampman district of southeastern Saskatchewan, and we were all played out from running and cavorting with our cousins on their farms. I envied my sisters propped against each other beside me, and my brother leaned against the window on the other side. They seemed to be able to fall asleep before we hit cruising speed. I was always too excited to be viewing the landscape and usually too anxious, even when the darkness enveloped us. My parents' conversation that night did nothing to settle me.

"Len ..." worried my mother, "do you have enough gas to get us home?" Mother came by her epithet, "Worrywart," quite honestly. Unfortunately, I took most of my cues from her.

"I'll pull into the next town." my father reassured her. "We've been bucking a strong headwind all the way."

My uncle had offered to fill the tank on the farm before we left with the cheaper, tax-free gasoline that was kept for use in farm vehicles. It was dyed purple so that the local constabulary could easily spot it with a quick check.

Use in personal automobiles was against the law. Dad had declined, likely due to the anxiousness expressed by my mother on a previous trip—of course transferred to me in multiples. She and I were certain we would spend the rest of our lives in jail for that malfeasance!

The road seemed to lengthen after my parents' exchange and it seemed like an hour—likely only minutes—before the sign announcing "Lajord 1" hove into view. I settled a bit but still perched with white knuckles clenching the back of the front bench seat. Dad pulled into the first gravel approach and seemed to follow it for some time. The dim misaligned headlights provided little help—one creating a pool of light just in front of the car, the other seemingly on antiaircraft duty. Finally, something appeared ahead in the one useful headlight's pale effect. It was the grade and bright orange and brown closed entrance to a grain elevator. He had taken a wrong turn!

My heart's now tympanic beat, I am certain, was audible to all. Mom only gasped, louder than was necessary, as Dad manoeuvred the car back from whence we came. Dad said nothing, but it seemed his usual casual grip on the steering wheel had tightened considerably. After we found the highway once again, we discerned that the hamlet of Lajord had no gasoline for sale. Dad then eased the Meteor back up to a reasonable, if somewhat reduced, speed.

Prairie towns were former service stops for the railways and consequently almost exactly nine miles apart. The next town was Kronau, and in my mind, it may as well have been on the other side of the planet. The time just crawled until we pulled into the next settlement and stopped at a service station's gas pumps. There were no lights on, but Dad went around the back of the station where the proprietor's living quarters were attached. I am not certain what entreaties he made, but soon Dad came back, together with the clearly dishevelled owner in tow. All he would have needed do was to have shown him the tears welling in my eyes, or Mom's pallor.

We were soon appropriately sated with fuel, and the return to highway speed seemed to illicit an annoyed grunt from my sleeping brother. My mother's silence, however, was deafening. While she held my younger sister a little bit more securely, her disquiet permeated the car. Dad seemed to know better than to address her directly, but I think he felt that he needed to restore some normalcy as he spoke, "That wasn't too bad …"

Len could see the plume rising nearly level with the aircraft from the smoldering target behind them. One lonely searchlight probed morosely nearby, occasionally highlighting the column of smoke—not that you needed it in the light of this scarcely waning full moon. He knew he should look for fighters, but he was drawn to the devastation that they had rained down upon this pretty landscape. He could still see occasional flashes as the bombers that had straggled unleashed their own malevolent, if tardy, torrents. It was obvious that some incendiaries had set the surrounding forest ablaze. What must it be like to endure that onslaught?

It was his sixth sortie with 158 Squadron, and the target for tonight was the Schneider Armament Works in Le Creusot, France. Len had wondered if they would ever get a so-called piece-of-cake target, and in his first trip that was not over Germany, this now seemed to be it. At briefing they had been told that this was the "Krups of France." Harkening to that heavily defended industrial target in the Ruhr was too recent a memory for him. They had just gone on a raid to its neighbour in "Happy Valley," Bochum, during the previous week. That one had nearly put the wind up him.

This trip had been a milk run in comparison. Of course, Barry and David taking them over that flak ship in the Channel on the way in to France was something he'd make certain he'd give them hell for back on the ground. But the flak seemed inaccurate and half-hearted. It had been quiet ever since. Barry was a wonderful skipper, and his piloting, Len reckoned, had gotten them out of plenty of scrapes. David was the navigator, and he had been their surrogate big brother since they crewed up together at OTU. He was ten years older than both and had the air of someone even more experienced. He exuded everything Len admired about the English—subtle humour, refined taste, and quiet confidence. Len felt like a bumpkin in his presence, but David—he could never bring himself to call him "Dave"—would never give him any evidence to feel that way. His navigation, from Len's backward perch in the rear turret and limited expertise in such matters, seemed as flawless as his character. There would have been no way for him to know the location of that flak ship beforehand, but Len would overlook that detail, as he planned to demand David's penance in buying the first round when they got back.

Barry was a different matter. Len and Barry were the same age and although thousands of miles, diverse cultures, and an ocean separated their pre-war worlds, they'd been like brothers since they met. It was the two of them together who had wandered about during the crewing exercise, choosing likely mates for them to sally forth with and share their fortunes. They had previously decided that navigation would be primary to their success and survival. Barry knew this from his much longer and detailed training as a pilot. Len felt this way because the mathematics involved in this arcane discipline was what had had him choose to be a gunner in the first place. And with that they had ambled to the quiet, older David and started to chat with this would-be Magellan. It seemed that many crews had already walked past the unassuming navigator, likely mistaking his gentlemanly reticence as aristocratic aloofness. No-one wanted a snob on their crew, but shortly into their easy banter, Len knew that Barry would be asking David to join them. Their concurrence was unspoken.

The rest of the original five men for their Wellington bomber crew at the No. 20 Operational Training Unit at Lossiemouth proceeded unremarkably. They collected their air bomber, Vick, and then chose the always-grinning lad whom they'd only ever call "Boots" as their wireless operator. While both these trades were of critical importance to their crew, one could easily grow into them and become proficient and so taking them, sight-unseen, seemed to be no issue. Barry told Len later than he had faith in the RAF's ability to turn out professionals. He knew that he could lead this crew.

And lead them he did. Len didn't know for certain if it was this way with all crews, but Barry was the man in charge when they were in the aircraft and in the air. The crew knew it, seemingly innately, for there was never any question. No one need be reminded of it with a dressing down and never did his directives receive a smart "Yes, sir!" as is so often the cliché depicted. A quick and confident "Aye, Skipper" was all he ever wanted and invariably got in acknowledgment to his orders. It struck Len a bit incongruous that this was the same man with whom he so easily and frequently matched pints at the Brunswick in Brid—until one or the other needed to be supported to their transport by the always attendant David.

"Crew check," came crackling from Len's headset, roughly jerking him from his reverie. It had been quiet for several minutes since they had turned for home, and while the fires burning from the shattered target factories still glowed miles behind them, the plume of smoke that had risen to likely eight or nine thousand feet was no longer easily discernible, even with the bright moonlight. Barry liked a defined order in this check-in, starting with the gunners and then with the crew in the forward part of the aircraft.

"Gunners?"

"Check, Skipper," replied Len first. It made sense for the more critical eyes to be checked in first—most bombers were attacked from behind, but Len had been, ostensibly, part of the "crew" for longest, so he reckoned that that was also part of the defined procedure.

"Still with you, Skip," was the easy, quick response from Rollie, the man in the mid-upper turret. They had picked up Rollie when they began conversion onto the four-engined Halifax bomber at RAF Rufforth, Heavy Conversion Unit—the previously flown Wellington had only the one true gun turret in the rear of the aircraft. Len got along well with him. Yes, they shared the same trade, but more significantly, on this crew, Rollie was the only man who could adequately contest putting down a yard of ale with Len.

"Navigator?"

"Aye, Skipper," came David's calm reply.

"Bomb aimer?"

"Watching the scenery, Skipper," said Vick laconically. Len smiled to himself. He knew that although the most critical part of Vick's work was done when the bomb had been released, he was still very busy with associated other chores, including his role now as the back-up navigator.

"W/Op?"

Silence. Barry waited a few beats and then a few decibels louder came, "Wireless operator, intercom check!"

Len could imagine some frantic shuffling up ahead when, finally, the intercom hissed, and the exaggerated alertness of Boots' voice fair shouted, "Aye aye, Captain!"

Len envisioned the twinkle in Barry's eyes as he paused to form his rebuke. "This isn't the RN, wireless operator; one 'aye' is sufficient. You weren't asleep, were you?"

Boots' reply could almost be predicted, "Just resting my eyes, Skipper."

"Engineer?"

Barry enquired of the last to hit the roll. "Right behind you, Skip," said Harry, the other man the crew had picked up in Rufforth. Harry was a wizard with the mechanics of this kite. He knew it like the back of his hand. His liaison with the ground crew was equal to the skipper's, and his genuine feel for what was necessary to keep the aircraft running was a more than welcome complement to the crew. Even though this was an airplane that they had not yet taken on operations, everything seemed, from Len's limited perspective, to be going well.

Barry had pranged their usual kite, *A for Able*, on a rather hairy landing after a bombing detail earlier this week. Somehow, two engines on that training run had decided to pack up during what was planned to be a proficiency exercise. When the first engine went unserviceable, Barry and Harry had gotten it feathered and turned back to Lissett, the detail cancelled. When the second engine, obviously not used to the extra strain, decided it had had enough near the 'drome, the landing was going to be an adventure. The Mark II of the Halifax was never overpowered to begin with and with two engines out, it had the flying characteristics of a set of car keys. Barry had gotten them down safely, but the aircraft would be out of service for a few weeks for repair. The incident might have shaken the confidence in the equipment, but the stature, in the crew's eyes of those who managed that shaky do so well—Barry and to a lesser extent, Harry—was never higher.

They flew on in silence. Len continued his survey of the sky. He divided his view into octals, and through a systematic pattern, checked each in turn. Barry banked the aircraft from time to time as well to help his view beneath. Len would stand up at these times and peer as far down as the limited space would accommodate. The moon was a mixed blessing tonight. He could see forever, it seemed, but that meant that they also could be seen. Still, if there was to be combat, it was likely far below them.

Barry had gone slightly off script on his planned route. He told them at dispersal that he planned to fly this one at over 10,000 feet. They were told at briefing that there would be light defences and that they should likely attack from minimum altitude—below 6000 was suggested. Barry didn't like the sound of that and had an innate fear of having things dropped on him from above. He told the crew that he'd likely keep it higher than the briefed altitude all the way and, indeed, Vick had put their load on the target from 10,000 feet. All were in support of the skipper on this; it made good sense.

That decision seemed to be further confirmed when Vick, likely again doing his erstwhile sightseeing, reported light flak and an aircraft hit far below as they were nearing the Normandy coast of France. Barry chimed in, "I saw it. Looks like a Halifax. It's on fire and spinning in." And then to the rest of the crew, but likely especially to the gunners, "Keep your eyes skinned, lads, we're not home yet!" Len and Rollie, with appropriate attention and alacrity, reported in turn, "Aye!" Their vigilance redoubled. Len was thankful for the greater altitude. There was no use sucking around for a dose of ack-ack if you could avoid it.

A few hyper-vigilant minutes passed before Len could make out the coastline of France. The breakers on the beach below were unmistakable in the clear moonlight. They were certainly not out of the woods yet, but it was comforting to see the continent receding. The intercom once again drew his attention.

"Skipper, our fuel consumption is a bit high," Harry reported from his gauges.

Barry did not reply to the engineer but called to David, "Navigator, I have 180 Indicated on the clock. What do you make our speed to be?"

There was a lengthening pause that was likely occasioned by David checking his calculations before he finally spoke, "Nowhere near that, Skipper. We are not off track at all, but I estimate our speed to be 135."

Barry reacted immediately, "That's a hell of a head wind. Bloody Met!"

Len paid little attention to the meteorological briefing before an op and it now seemed that they had not created any fans on this crew tonight. There was at least a moment or two of silence, as Len imagined that Barry was giving some time for the engineer to make his calculations. It stretched on interminably before the captain's voice asked the question they all desperately wanted answered: "Engineer, have we got enough juice?"

Harry replied matter-of-factly, "We'll see Blighty again, Skip, but the base is long odds."

There was an almost palpable silence on the intercom. All too clearly now, Len realized the downside of their high-altitude gambit, as it was likely apparent to the entire crew. Maintaining higher altitude cost you petrol, and running into stronger winds at altitude robbed your airspeed. They were briefed that their op would be long—seven hours at the extreme, and they were bombed up and fuelled accordingly. No one foresaw the winds they were now fighting. The pitch of the engine's drone shifted slightly as, no doubt, Barry sought lower wind speeds beneath them through a gentle glide to lower altitude. This would also reduce fuel consumption, but they had sinned, and the laws of physics and fuel use could absolve them of only so much.

Time always seemed to stretch in the least favorable way. As the English coastline slipped beneath his turret, Len was sure that hours had passed since they learned of their critical fuel situation. A check of his watch in the glow of his turret's reflector sight showed that they had been airborne for more than six hours. It was becoming increasingly unlikely that he would see his own bunk tonight. Another fear now gripped him as he surveyed the landscape bathed in the light of this night's ever-present moon. Over the land there was the unmistakable ethereal opacity of ground fog over most of what he surveyed. A knot tightened in his stomach. He thought, *Some milk run!*

The Merlin engines on the bomber always made a drone that was better felt than heard. As long as their reassuring vibration was present, you could feel at relative ease. Here in the extreme tail end of the aircraft, movements and vibrations were magnified. Len could sense Barry's skillful management of the power governed by the throttles. He was confident in his skipper's ability to land this kite—if they could find an airfield that was not socked in by fog. They were still high enough now that if the fuel ran out, most might still be able to parachute, but that was a ropey prospect at best.

Len could hear the chatter on the intercom as Barry asked Boots to canvass for an open airfield. The wireless operator reported back at intervals, but it seemed that most of the southern half of England was inaccessible for landing. Apparently, it was clear farther north. That was perfect news for any crew without a shortage of petrol, but it did this lot little good. There was almost nothing to distract Len now they were over home soil. Attack by enemy fighters was not impossible but unlikely, so his responsibilities were less critical. All he could do now is trust in his crewmates. He crossed himself and started to pray.

"Harwell says they're marginal but open, Skipper," Boots reported from his station in a tone that seemed oddly like imploring relief.

"I did beam approach circuits and bumps there in an Oxford. It's a Wimpy base now. It will do nicely." Barry's lilting offhand reply came reassuringly on the 'com. "Navigator, give me a course," he continued cheerily. Len knew Barry's pilot training had taken him all over Britain, but Len did not recall hearing of this station in any of his good mate's tales. That Barry knew the 'drome was very good news. That it was at least able to accommodate Wellingtons—affectionately known to all and sundry as the "Wimpy"—was icing on the cake. They only needed their gas to hold out.

There was very little patter on the intercom now as Len watched the gauze-draped landscape cascade beneath him. There were breaks in the ground fog that he could see, but they seemed few and far between. They were descending slowly, and the propellers continued their rhythmic chop of the air. He was entirely accustomed to this backward view of what they had already passed. Seeing what was ahead only seemed to make him more anxious. He once swapped seats with Rollie on an air test, and they both had been more than happy to get back to their usual seats. The view from the mid-upper turret was *too* scenic! The encroaching fog was not deep, but from his oblique perspective, it seemed to be getting more widespread.

If Barry could see the runway, Len was certain he could land it smooth as glass. What was out of his control, however, was the constantly dwindling petrol supply. There was complete trust in what his crew could do. Barry could land a threshing machine if it had wings. Harry would find every dram of juice the tanks would offer and manage all the power. David would give them the most direct course possible. It is always the things that were beyond control that seemed to make your heart beat faster. And it made Len more earnest in his continued prayer. At any moment the engines might sputter for want of gas. Every slight misfire—and there were always plenty in these engines—might be the start of their unpowered glide into the lush green English countryside.

Len felt the gear come down. The aerodynamics changed considerably, and he felt the airplane buffet and shudder, but the engines were still driving the lumbering crate. If they cut out now, it would not be pretty. "Please, Lord, carry my mates home …" came the whisper that only God might hear. They were terminally low now, and the familiar sight of the runway threshold slipped beneath his turret and he finally exhaled. The thump of the gear and the puff of rubber smoke that heralded every landing were almost anticlimactic. They were down in what Barry always called another "controlled crash." The station was unfamiliar, and they would, no doubt, be scrounging for something to eat and a place to nod off, but it was all small potatoes now. He crossed himself one more time and glanced fractionally skyward—where he knew both threat and sanctuary lay.

5

I could smell the sweetness of the white, vaguely heaped mass in the bowl before me. I stared at it suspiciously as a cat might eye a strange new toy. I was not going to be fooled by the empty plates and utensils licked nearly clean by my long-since departed siblings. It was just me and this unfamiliar dessert left here at the chrome set table in my parents' kitchen where we always ate our evening meals. Dad was still here too, sitting at his familiar spot at the head of the table, and Mom was skittering around preparing for the long ordeal of cleaning pots and dishes after the meal. It was only a matter of time before this stand-off would play out, and I suspected that it would not be a tidy ending.

"Mark, are you going to eat your rice pudding?" Mother's accusation drew no response from me for several seconds, but I finally reached for my spoon, though I now wished I had slunk from the table with the rest of my family in the hopes that the blame could be spread. But it was too late for that gambit, and my traitorous siblings had finished every last morsel at their places. Desserts were not a common occurrence in our house. I wondered how long I could clutch my still spoon before this stall would be uncovered as well.

"You know I spent most of the afternoon making that, so govern yourself accordingly," warned my mother. I am certain that I was the only five-year-old who understood what that phrase meant, but I also knew the dangers of not heeding its inferred consequences. My father sat impassively, apparently engrossed after the meal in whatever he was reading in his carefully quarter-folded newspaper, seemingly content to allow this to play out without his intervention. I extended my spoon into the almost unyielding clot and procured what I felt was a sufficient amount to appease the glare that burned into me and moved it cautiously toward my lips. This seemed to placate Mom and she turned to continue fussing about her chores.

The spoon and its contents paused only briefly as the sweet smell assaulted my nostrils and duplicitously encouraged me to put the pudding in my mouth. Pulling the spoon back, the lump languished on my tongue. The texture and weight made me rue my decision to even attempt this. Did I really take this much on my spoon? Was the bolus getting larger? Was it moving! I held it my mouth for as long as I could, but I could not suppress the inevitable gag reflex, nor the almost imperceptible click that it creates, but I finally choked it down my throat.

At the sound, Mom turned and started to wipe her hands ominously on her apron. The scene had not escaped Dad's attention, and he seemed to catch her eye with a slight turn of his head. Their eyes met and in the volumes that a glance can convey between two people so obviously in tune, he simply shook his head slightly and her demeanor softened. She stared for a moment and then sighed heavily, "Okay, go!"

I bolted from the table, leaving the vile dessert behind. I have subsequently tried rice pudding, but I can honestly say that I have never enjoyed it. There was no explaining my visceral reaction to the texture of the pudding that day, nor my continued avoidance. There was something almost innate about it, as if there was some buried memory or traumatic previous experience for which there is simply no explanation.

The hut was cold as it always seemed to be recently. Although it was dark, Len could not sleep. He laid still for fear that the slightest movement would disturb the frail cocoon of warm air that this rough blanket had managed to trap near his body. In the darkness, he heard the cacophony of snores and wheezes from his fellow *kriegies*. If one listened closely, you could make out the individuals making the drone. Some were sonorous snores while others were a light, raspy rale. Still others could be heard just sleeplessly breathing, as Len seemed destined to spend this night doing.

They were packed in this hut like sardines, thought Len. He then immediately regretted that culinary reference. It had been months since he had had anything resembling a full meal. Even a sardine would be a treat. Now he rued all the complaints he had made regarding what the mess back at RAF Lissett turned out. How he would heap complaints upon the poor WAAF staff for the lack of imagination that created a constantly congealed offering of greasy, fried mystery meats and the only vegetable the British seemed to be able to cultivate—brussels sprouts. The girls, though, gave as good as they got. Any complaint was met with a tart riposte from those uniformed birds, and you were left speechless looking at the south end of a WAAF travelling north.

The image of those well-turned calves now filled his reverie, and that was even worse than imagining sardines, Spam, or sprouts!

Len shivered again. It was only late August. Why was he so chilled? Yes, he had a persistent cough, but they all did. It was understandable with all the tobacco that they smoked. Cigarettes seemed to be one of the few things of which they had sufficient supply. Even when they were forced from *Stalag Luft VI* in Heydekrug by the advancing Russians, what they first thought to bring was their stock of cigarettes. After all, cigarettes were currency, recreation, and comfort. They carried all they could from their former home and they simply burned the rest in a comforting bonfire. Better that than have the goons get them. The warmth of that fire was something he could certainly use now.

They had left Heydekrug in such a hurry. Len wondered what became of the tomato plants he had so carefully tended back in their garden there. Had they borne fruit? Had his careful pruning and staking been taken up by someone else? Did some Russian soldier get the benefit of his husbandry? Well, he was certain that they would have appreciated the garden more than the cans of powdered milk, *Klim* ("milk" spelled backwards), that they had left behind—some with foot powder substituted for the original white, granular contents. Len chuckled inwardly at that bit of cheeky sabotage. All's fair in love and war!

But the trip to their new home here in Pomerania was not fair. It was hell. Weeks of forced marches and cramped conveyances—boxcars and ship's holds—landed them here in *Stalag Luft IV*, a shoddily and hastily constructed camp carved out of the forest near Gross Tychow in northeastern Germany. Here, the huts were drafty and there was no heating provided. Len couldn't imagine what would happen when it inevitably turned cold outside.

Things had grown steadily worse for Len since that night he and his crew were forced to bail out of their damaged Halifax after taking flak over Berlin. The skipper, Robbie, had done his best to try to get back to 158 Squadron's base in Yorkshire, but ordered them out over Holland when it was apparent that they'd never make it back across the North Sea in their badly shot up aircraft. Len's hand and legs had been injured when the shell exploded under his turret. Now he unconsciously balled his left fist and felt the chunk of shrapnel still lodged in the flesh near the base of his thumb. His own wounds had healed, but everything external to him in this great adventure had continued to worsen.

All signs pointed to the war not going in favour of his captors. Their speedy abandonment of *Stalag Luft VI* ahead of the encroaching Eastern Front and the carefully transcribed BBC Radio reports received on a wireless concealed in an adjacent hut told him much of what he needed to know. The greatly reduced supply of provisions and interminable delays in even the requisite Red Cross support told the rest. It was of little comfort that the *kriegies* knew that their side would be victorious—they were still captive and held at the whim of personnel who may have little to lose. Surely there would be even more difficult days ahead.

Another chill wracked Len's body. It was becoming obvious that he would get no more sleep this night. Perhaps if he got an early start, he might avoid the crush at the latrines that seemed to come later. Unlike the comparatively luxurious accommodations in Heydekrug, this prison camp offered very little for personal care. There was one spot for the 200 odd airmen in this hut. But still, to beat the rest to the "aborts" and get his lavatory business done would surely put a rosier glow on yet another dismal day. He quietly slunk from his upper slot in the double-deck bunk.

He was not the only one stirring at this time, for he could make out at least one other form moving in the peri-dawn murk inside the hut. That shape seemed to have the steady gait of a long-term *kriegie*. Perhaps it was strange, but you could certainly discern the careful tread of a newcomer from those whose movements reeked of resignation. Len idly wondered when he, himself, had made that transition. He started his steady shuffle to the abort he hoped would be deserted.

He soon realized that his chosen path would put him on collision course in the narrow aisle between bunks with the other man, so he instinctively slowed to either greet or dodge the man. The target did not veer from its course, so Len made further room, feeling that the man had perhaps not seen him. As they drew closer, Len tried to make eye contact. He knew everyone in this hut—perhaps not as intimately as he knew Robbie, Hale, and Lofty, his crewmates from 158—but most were, at least, Canadians. As they passed closely, the vacant stare of "Hap" Halpin seemed to burn into the space behind Len's accommodating dodge. They passed without words or acknowledgement.

Hap, like Len, was another RCAF air gunner, but he had bailed out from his stricken Wellington in late 1942 and had been shuffled from *Stalag* to *Stalag* ever since. The rest of the crew of his Wimpy were unaccounted for, and that seemed to set him a bit twitchy from the outset. It had only gotten worse. Len suspected that his nickname may have started as an abbreviation of his surname, but was now certainly reflective of his increasingly "wire-happy" state. He was a man most tended to avoid for fear of setting him off, but his nationality led him naturally to this particular hut in which most of the minority population of Canadians in *Stalag Luft IV* had agglomerated.

Len continued his quest for ablution and smiled inwardly at his personal turn of phrase, but the activity and long hours of sleeplessness now made his need for relief more urgent. The encounter with Hap had made him again feel guilty for leaving his good friends from his crew in their own hut and joining this largely Canadian group. Aircrew were closer than brothers in that each knew that they were alive each day because of their common, intersecting duty. It was always that way with bomber crews and because of that, most everyone understood cases such as Hap. But flying days were long over for most of them and the increasingly long period of captivity had shown that they really were from different worlds.

Most of the blokes from Len's crew were English and had distinctively English interests. They talked endlessly about soccer— "football" they called it. Or else they were playing it. It was clear from even the least talented of them that they had all been well-versed in it from when they were in diapers, so Len's pitiful attempts at the sport were embarrassing to all except for maybe Hap. Len had to fight the urge to pick up the ball and run with it—the way that proper football is played! No, he was much more comfortable discussing hockey or baseball with his compatriots. And so the pull of sharing quarters with his countrymen was too great. He still saw and spent long hours with his former crewmates, but he felt more at home here in "Maple Leaf Garden," as they had sardonically dubbed their hut.

The only Canadians that were on Len's last flight were now either in different camps or of fate unknown. Pappy, the navigator, was an officer so likely went to *Stalag Luft III*. At least Len hoped that he made it there. Pappy was Jewish and had frequently joked back at Lissett that he didn't anticipate great longevity if he was ever captured by the Nazis. The other Canuck on board was the replacement gunner, Slim, whom no one had seen since they parted at the escape hatch while parachuting from their badly damaged bomber.

Len found the facilities as empty as he had hoped, and some quiet solitude was expected at least until the rest had roused and slipped into their enforced routine. Recalling his erstwhile crewmate, Slim, gave him reason to consider the matter in more depth. He realized that he hadn't thought of that man in months. Of course, he and the others wondered what had become of him, but it seemed that the war was filled with people you met and then never saw again. One instant, you were locked in a life or death struggle together, and then the next, you were quaffing down a few pints with them. And then it seemed that just another moment later, that person was snatched from you—by duty elsewhere, hopefully, or more likely by grim operational circumstance. And you so seldom knew the outcome. All that was left was the latent guilt in that you had become accustomed to this happening.

Len made his way back to his bunk, still pondering the vagaries of his life. At least it kept his mind off his empty stomach. By the time he got to his rack, most people had at least awakened, and there was a general stir in the now-brighter morning light. Folks just moving around seemed to take some of the chill off, and he was very pleased to find that someone had gotten some hot water started. There was a steaming *Klim* can on the makeshift table near the bunks, so Len set about rummaging in his meagre possessions for one of the few D-bars he still had left. He was still whittling chocolate flakes into the water to make their morning watery, vaguely-cocoa brew—what would pass as their breakfast. Stu, the man who had procured the water, sidled back from the idle conversation he was having with a few of the others.

"G'mornin', Len. Back from your morning constitutional, I see." Stu's easy manner and bulky frame were a comfort to all who knew him. He, like the rest, had probably lost a quarter to a third of his fighting weight while in captivity, but he was still an imposing figure. His broad shoulders and stone hands were always welcome in your company as you encountered the occasional fractious episode in camp. His size was usually enough to keep the peace, but if push ever came to shove, you might actually fell him with about the fifth blow of a sledge hammer. His rural background, hailing from a family ranching operation in southern Alberta, gave them an instant commonality.

"Thanks for fetching the water, Stu. The cocoa'll be ready in a sec."

Len stirred the thin, brown brew with the improvised implement that he had fashioned from the remnants of a tin that once contained corned beef. Almost everything they used had been jury-rigged from one Red Cross parcel or another, and this one was no different. Necessity had always been the mother of invention. Surviving the Great Depression in rural Saskatchewan was the perfect preparation for these lean days in captivity—the combination of ingenuity and collaboration was the perfect strategy then as it was now.

Len offered the first swig of his creation to Stu, who took a cautious draught and smacked his lips appreciatively. "Mighty fine, Len, mighty fine!" he lied and then passed it back. Len took his own slurp and at once wished he had put in more chocolate shavings. But he knew, as they all did, that they never knew when the next Red Cross parcels would arrive. There had been a long interruption in their delivery after the move from Heydekrug, and when they did start once again arriving, their distribution was not as regular. They all much preferred the chocolate "D-bars" that the Americans got—the taste was much better—and so what Len had procured had cost him his ration of jam.

"Pukka gen from the boys over there," Stu tossed his head in the direction of the men with whom he was just talking, "is that there was a new shipment of *kriegies* overnight. Most are Yanks, but there's a few RAF and 'colonials'." Stu spat out the last word with his usual sarcasm. He still smarted from some comments crudely cast his way from the worst of the aristocratic RAF officer caste he had encountered in his service. Len had had very few such experiences, likely traced to his serving and proving himself in an RAF squadron. Stu's only service was in the wholly Canadian Group 6 of Bomber Command. Perhaps integration softened such attitudes. In any case, Len had learned not to argue the issue.

"Maybe we'll meet 'em after morning *appell*," Len offered simply. Long gone were the days when the new captives were paraded from the main gate into the camp. The resulting commotion was almost a free-for-all, and order was difficult to maintain. The goons had more recently made much less ceremony of the regular, sad influx.

Still, it was always an event to get newcomers. Although they were often full of trepidation and anxiety, it broke the monotony of captivity to show them the routines and conventions. Plus, once they began to trust the old heads, they brought welcome and refreshing glimpses of the world outside the wire. Some of it could even be believed.

The warm, brown liquid Len drank did little to quell the pangs in his still-empty stomach. There was the promise of some usually stale bread after daily routine of morning prisoner roll call—*appell*, as Jerry called it. *The same thing we called it in French*, he mused. Len was defiant in resisting using any German words or expressions, except when he could get some perverse satisfaction from it. Believing that the expression likely had a French root gave him that pyrrhic pleasure.

Len sat on his bunk and thought of all the French he had cleverly forgotten in his life. That was all they spoke when he was growing up on the farm, but the bitter truth of knowing so little English when he first started school stung to his core. He worked very hard to pick it up, and he fought to hide his linguistic shortcomings—so much so that he and his siblings often eschewed their heritage by opting to pronounce their surnames the way the local anglophones did, and consequently denying their Quebec roots. Len even claimed knowing little French on his RCAF Enlistment Attestation. He had practiced very long to lose any residual accent but still struggled with some words containing the difficult "th" sound. He chose to simply avoid them. Being in England, and especially in an RAF squadron, was a godsend—there was such a variety of accents there that he could simply blend in and not have to watch his speech. Some of the old insecurities had reappeared since he had chosen to join the Canadians in this barracks, but they all had much larger problems than the nuances of language.

The murmur engendered by the morning routine started to grow into a din as heard above the noise were the shouts of, "*Raus! Raus!*" from the goons. It was time for *appell*. They all got to their feet and started their practiced movement, with dubious alacrity, to the square outside their hut. It was a nice August morning and the chill Len felt last night had finally dissipated, though the weary exhaustion remained. The sudden influx of fresh outside air evoked a deep cough that left a sharp pain in his right chest. He was becoming certain that he might be getting sick.

The *kriegies* fell into practised and familiar ranks of five outside their barracks with Len near the back of one such row. That they stood smartly was not so much in deference to their captors but in esprit d'corps. They were not going to give any indication that they had been broken. The predominantly British occupants of the next building stood in similarly formed order in plain view near them. Len knew where to look to catch the eye of his crewmates and made quick eye contact with both Robbie and Hale. He could not spot Lofty, but given the latter's diminutive stature, that wasn't unusual. Faint nods and smiles passed between the friends.

The German NCOs started their count. It was largely perfunctory, since this was still a new camp, and the "X"—meaning "escape"—infrastructure was not well-established. Both prisoner and guard knew this. There had been many more plans afoot in the previous camp with elaborate roles, duties, and equipment. That was one outgrowth of being in a new camp—the prisoners seemed as disorganized as the goons.

The count soon seemed to be finished, and lack of anything untoward was evidenced by the absence of excitement as the final tallies were made. The prisoners stood at loose attention and waited to be dismissed from *appell* when an announcement was made that there were new Commonwealth POWs. Coincident was the appearance of maybe a dozen blue uniforms marching in single file to be stood between the denizens of Maple Leaf Garden on one side and the RAF blokes on the other. Len spotted one deeper blue tunic—an Aussie—so they were likely to gain another bunkmate. His keen eyes also picked out the unmistakable shoulder flashes of "CANADA" on at least one other new arrival. The view of the rest was impeded, but there would be plenty of time to scope out the new boys. He looked forward to meeting them, even though it meant they'd be even more crowded in their hut.

"Let's go introduce ourselves to the new lot," said Stu as the guards scurried off to their usual posts. "There looked to be a few new Canucks."

Len grunted in assent. He had no doubt of Stu's assessment, given the perspective that his more generous stature afforded. Several small groups had formed around the new internees. Usually, assembly of more than three or four bodies brought stern guttural warnings from the goons, but they had been known to understandably relax this edict when there was an influx of new aircrew. Generally, the greeting of new men was a quick handshake and the same repeated questions about hometown and other banalities. Anything more detailed could certainly wait—at least until the newcomer could be confirmed as a genuine article and not some ferret plant of the *Abwehr*—or of other German security organizations.

Len and Stu met one flight sergeant from British Columbia who seemed likeable if a bit twitchy. He seemed to be favouring a shoulder and likely had had a rough time getting out of his aircraft. At least he had gotten out. They then drifted to the one other new Canadian, and as they approached from the port quarter, Len thought there was something familiar about his voice and manner. As they drew abreast, the man turned and extended his hand by rote. Len saw his eyes widen and jaw drop in abject shocked recognition—he was certain that his own expression was a mirror image.

"Nick! You silly ol' bugger!" Len grabbed his proffered hand and pumped it enthusiastically. "Who the hell did you brown off this time to be sent to this arsehole of a camp!"

Nick's face had recovered some of its devil-may-care nonchalance. "Just the usual gang of muckety-mucks. They sent me to check up on *your* latest

SNAFU." Len could not peel the grin from his face while he kept shaking the hand of his closest ally at Initial Training in Toronto.

"I'm going to need that back by lunchtime," Nick said simply, looking down at the apparent death grip that Len had on his hand. "When *is* chow? I haven't eaten since yesterday."

Len sheepishly let the hand fall from his grip and looked sidelong at Stu, who had been silent throughout this rare reunion of mates. The raised eyebrows they exchanged conveyed all that was needed, and Nick simply fell into silent contrition at his obvious misspeak about food. Nick then turned to the man who was obviously Len's companion and offered his hand.

"Nick, this is my bunkmate, Stu," Len said with more formality than was necessary. "Nick was my buddy at ITS before we were encouraged into other trades." The two exchanged greetings. "Stu ... we gotta get Nick into our block. We gotta talk to the skipper!"

Usually there was a good deal of sorting that took place with new *kriegies*. Care had to be taken to weed out potential ferrets and unsuitable matches. But it was rare that someone came in for whom another *kriegie* could so completely vouch that this was certain to be a special case. Len and Stu would talk to the senior man in the barracks—the block skipper. Rank did not determine who the skipper was—he was essentially elected and was ironically a signal product of democratic process in this travesty of democracy, a Nazi German prison of war camp. Len had some seniority and was trusted, so his word would carry weight with the man in charge. He was certain that they would find room for Nick in their building.

It only took most of the morning for Len to drag Nick around to get him kitted up for their building and to introduce him to most of the regulars. It would take a bit more time to catch up with him and to prise some of the details of how they ended up back together. It had been just over a year since they last hoisted a few in Toronto before going their separate ways. Len recalled that he was at first disappointed that they had lost touch, but that was early in their respective service careers. Now Len knew that it was rare to again find an old friend, so he cherished this moment and it gave him hope, perhaps fatuously, that he could reconnect with all those he once thought were as close—or closer. He tried to push the faces of those whom he knew for certain he'd never see again in this life to the back recesses of his memory.

Len also introduced Nick to the long queue that formed far too infrequently when the goons were distributing what meagre rations captives might be afforded. Today's fare was what had become the usual—one piece of dark bread—about half a small loaf. They were cautioned by those distributing this that it was likely all they were to receive today. Back in the hut, Len shared some of the raisins from his last Red Cross parcel with Nick, along with the likely-rancid butter that he had left. Len even made another cup of his "D-bar coffee"—but only because of the celebratory mood he was in after finding an old friend. They made certain to keep some of their bread to accompany the evening meal—whatever else that might be. Stu had gone off to scrounge what he might find near the *Truppenlager*—the guards' barracks. The Germans too were feeling the food shortage, but they often discarded their waste where the *kriegies* might pick through their refuse. Stu was good at scrounging—it was likely the deterrence of his imposing size that dissuaded others from tussling over scraps—and usually he was able to find enough to supplement their diet with what the goons and their dogs wouldn't or couldn't eat.

After a time, they saw Stu enter the barracks with his massively large hands clutching some ill-gotten booty to his chest. "Oh, we'll eat like the King himself tonight, boys!" he proudly exclaimed as he dumped his treasure into a large, crudely constructed pot. They used this vessel to concoct the stews and soups that were made of all manner of dribs and drabs that they might donate or scrounge.

They simmered their cache—it had turned out to be potato and turnip peels—for the rest of the afternoon and added what few seasonings that could be garnered from a few depleted larders. In the dimming evening hours of this near autumn evening, they parcelled out their thin broth into whatever favourite, repurposed can they fancied. Nick followed Len, and they made their way back to where they had stored their rationed bread from earlier.

Len was dipping his bread as Nick examined the soup. "What are the white bits? Noodles or rice?" the newest *kriegie* asked earnestly.

"Rice," answered Len with equanimity, as he cast a barely discernible wink toward Stu.

"Oh … where'd you get the rice?" asked Nick, quite brightly but then trailed off in dawning comprehension. He could see as well as the others, even in this dim light, that the grains of "rice" were segmented and of a variety of lengths. Nick's face contorted as he gently but certainly put down his maggot-ridden soup can.

Len and the others shared a wry smile. They knew, as Nick would soon, that this ersatz "rice" would be the only protein they consumed today, and they were not going to be denied that nutrition by thinking too much about it. Getting through today to tomorrow was always the goal. The quiet slurping continued.

6

I had to run to keep up with Dad's normally brisk walk as he breezed through the grass infield of our city's main athletic field. It was not that his pace was that quick, it was that his natural, long stride covered great distances in short order. I would walk for several very fast steps and break into a run to catch up. Dad did not hold my hand, but I always got the sense that he knew exactly where I was—and he understood that I knew better than to fall too far behind.

It was a sunny Saturday morning in June—late in the school year, but this was the traditional time for the city-wide track and field competition for elementary schools in our city. In Saskatchewan, where winters often last until mid-April or later, the outside athletic season had to be squeezed into the few weeks between the snow's disappearance and the end of the school year at this month's end. My brother, Barry, was representing his school in this meet, and Dad never missed an opportunity to cheer on his children and, for that matter, all members of our school, for which he was a past-president of its Home and School Association, the equivalent of a PTA in many other places. This was Barry's last year in public school before he moved to the new high school and so this competition was almost a rite of passage.

Barry's name, I knew, was short for "Barrington," and I also knew that he was named for a pilot that my father had flown with during the war. I did not know very much about the original Barrington, save for the fact that he had been killed in action. That fact alone was enough to dissuade me from asking more.

We finally found Barry stooging about with several of his friends. I was uncertain of what his event might be, but was excited to be seeing my big brother compete because, as we all know, big brothers are always the very best at what they do. Some other kids seemed to be in the midst of taking turns throwing what seemed to be, from their difficulty in heaving it very far, a heavy metal ball. This must have been the "shot put" that I had seen in our set of encyclopaedias. My brother did not seem involved, so I hoped that he would be in one of the other events I had read about—the discus, or maybe even the javelin.

Dad and I moved to be out of the way, but not before we saw that Barry had seen us. He had ridden his bicycle to the venue earlier, so he was not beholden to us for his transportation. He was already thirteen years old—almost an adult! Soon there appeared to be some activity as a man holding what, in my mind, were several spears called out to the kids waiting that they were ready to begin.

My brother was going to throw the javelin! How neat was this?

Barry listened to instructions and then took his place second in line. Our surname near the beginning of the alphabet always meant an early start position. After watching the initial competitor's unexceptional attempt, it was soon Barry's turn. I watched as he sprinted, brandishing the spear like some caricature from an awful 1950s African adventure film. He suddenly stopped short and flung the javelin. It sailed through the air and spun slowly and majestically almost one-and-a-half times before planting itself backwards far short of even the previous competitor's modest toss. Even I could tell that this was far from a passable effort.

"Way to go, Barry!" my father bellowed. "Great throw!"

I just looked at Dad and saw his beaming face and thought of how wonderful it will feel in the future to have him that proud of me, too.

It was not usual for Len to sweat out take offs, but this time it appeared that they were finally going to start their operational tour. He could almost hear his heart beating through the many layers of clothes plus the Mae West that he wore, even above the steady drone of the idling Merlin engines. They say that you always remember your first, and it was true—his first trip at Bombing and Gunnery school in the rickety old *Fairey Battle* was something he would never forget. His heart was pounding then as it was now—two aspiring air gunner trainees crammed into the back of that dilapidated flying machine, set to show to all and sundry that they were to the Vickers gun what Billy Bishop had been to the RAF. That initial flight was ten months ago nearly to the day. Yesterday, it seemed like years ago. Now, all the old apprehension started to muster itself once again

Len looked at the lengthy line of idling Halifax bombers trailing them from his cramped seat in the rear turret of his own. They snaked their way behind him down the perimeter taxiway at Squadron 158's home here at RAF Lissett. In the dim light of this mid-May late evening, he could just make out the navigation lights of all those four-engine heavy bombers following his own—*G for George*—so it was natural to count them. There were eight. He recalled that from briefing, the squadron was sending twenty-one kites, likely a record number, so to his mounting superstitious horror he realized that they were to be the thirteenth to be airborne. What a way to start a tour!

Briefing had ordered all aircraft to be airborne by midnight, and a quick check of his watch told Len that they were right on schedule. He saw another kite start its lumbering ooze past in his peripheral vision. Down the runway Len watched it struggle until its shape was lost in the darkness that enveloped the base at this late hour—only from the glow of its departing navigation lights and the occasional flash from the inadequately damped exhausts of its Merlin engines could it still be seen climbing slowly. The lights would be soon extinguished, and the exhaust flames hopefully lessened with reduced strain, as the Halifax made every effort at stealth as it flew as a discrete part of the loosely concentrated swarm of bombers rendezvousing over their assigned target for tonight—Duisburg. Len always wondered just how stealthy they were as he routinely saw sparks flying past his rear turret on their many night-time training flights. Maybe his eyes were just more sensitive. He tried to not think about that as he noticed yet another bomber start its roll with the previous one still clearly in sight. Their turn would soon come.

"Lads, Brownie in *K for King* is next up, and we are right behind." Barry's calm voice broke several minutes of intercom silence. "Is everything okay?" Barry's informality in asking for a pre-flight check in from his crew was SOP—Standard Operating Procedure—but they all understood their response was dutifully required and in prescribed order. The pilot as captain of the aircraft would have it no other way.

"Rear turret, ok!" said Len first with more certainty than he felt. Rollie replied next from the other turret, and the others quickly all followed suit. The voices were all edged with anticipation—except, of course, for the imperturbable Boots at the wireless table, who seemed as excited by the prospect of his first operational flight as someone being offered a second cube of sugar for his tea. And Barry, of course, was cool and in control. The operation was his responsibility, and he wore it as if he'd been born to it.

Len felt the aircraft turn into position, and he was left peering into the near-total blackness of the fields and hedgerows surrounding the East Yorkshire countryside. The plane began to shake as Barry ran up the engines to maximum power to strain against the fully locked brakes of *G for George*.

"Okay, we've got 'green,' lads," said Barry as Len noticed movement. "Here we go."

Len could vaguely make out a sparse crowd clustered near the terminal truck waving to him and his companions. Some were waving franticly, some were waving by rote, and others were just watching impassively as he slipped past. He did not wave back—hoping that that showed he was calmly doing his duty. What really came to mind was whether they knew if he was coming back or not. Far too frequently, fewer came back than departed, and he wondered if the crowd was more "death watch" than "well-wishers." Len tried to keep a good thought—he did appreciate them being there; after all, it was very late.

The runway grew longer and longer behind him as Len centred his turret for the takeoff roll. The aerodynamics was best predicted when the turrets were unmoving and symmetrical, so the gunners did their part in giving Barry one less thing to worry about. Getting the Halifax airborne was always a dodgy proposition, for the airplane never just leapt into the air. Len was often thankful for his rearward facing view. He might not like seeing how little runway was left. He knew, however, when they were close, because the fixed tail wheel, just beneath him, was the first thing to leave the concrete.

Then the wings would be well on their way to having sufficient lift. Len remembered that much from early classes in flight dynamics. It was all up to the engines, aerodynamics, and Barry now, but still Len rambled off a quick Lord's Prayer. It could only help.

The rumble of tire rubber against pavement abruptly transitioned to the steady throb of the engines and whistling of the wind past the many open patches in the structure of Len's turret. Much of the sound was muted by the heavy accoutrements of his kit and the heavy earphones of his intercom headset, while the dark sky and blacked out countryside robbed him of any other clues to their speed; the sound provided the only gauge that they were indeed airborne and climbing. They were on their way. Finally, they were on their way.

It had been dark on the ground, but there was still some light and in the rapidly receding dimness of the aerodrome, Len could make out the few bombers that were still waiting to take off. They were disappearing now as his own gained speed and altitude. Now Barry banked *G for George* slowly. There were no sudden corrections, for they were now fully loaded with fuel, high explosives, and incendiaries. RAF Lissett was the bomber base closest to the North Sea—just a scant two miles from that cold expanse. The character of the air changed over the water, so while the low cloud through which they now flew obscured the surface, Len could tell that they had now left solid land behind. Barry and Harry, the flight engineer, were now busy trying to push the bomber higher and higher. The briefed bombing height was 19,000 feet, and every crew would struggle to get their kites there as soon as they could. It was always a certainty in aviation that altitude was easier to lose than to gain, so you wanted to put as much space between you and the ground as soon as possible. It only made sense to start the slow climb as close to the relative safety of English airspace as was possible.

It was getting colder and colder in the turret as the wind permeated the spaces left open to afford greatest visibility. Altitude also played havoc with temperature, and it routinely approached -50F. *Even colder than winter at home in Lampman, Saskatchewan,* Len thought, *and here it was mid-May.* He was thankful for his electrically heated flying suit, but still some parts were subject to the cold more than others. He moved his hands frequently to keep the circulation going. They were scheduled for at least five hours in this flying icebox. Heat, like height, was far easier lost than gained.

They finally broke through the cloud, and the waxing quarter moon became their most visible companion, but it was just now setting in the distance behind them and for this, Len was grateful. No sense in giving any added help to some enemy night fighter pilot. A few flashes could be seen in the sky around them, which might just be meteors but more likely other air gunners in the bomber stream testing their guns. Len was itching to test his from the moment they crossed the coast but wanted to wait until things had become less hectic for the other crew members after takeoff. Now was an appropriate time.

"Skipper," Len called after keying his intercom button, "okay to test guns?"

"Ok, gunners, make sure the path is clear," came Barry's easy reply. The admonishment was appreciated if superfluous—every gunner knew this standard operation procedure.

Len checked the direction he was going to shoot and squeezed off a short burst. The chatter of the guns so close was both heard and felt. What always surprised him was that the scent of expended cordite seeped in through his oxygen mask. He kept that fastened to his face for warmth even when flying below 10,000 feet—the usual altitude for its mandatory use. In short order he also sensed from the vibration that Rollie tested his twin Brownings in the mid-upper turret, but he missed seeing any tracer snaking from that station. Perhaps Rollie had hosed some out to the side.

Up to this point it had been like any other of dozens of training flights. Despite the anticipation and anxiety Len had felt on the ground tonight, he still had difficulty wrapping his head around the fact that this one was different. Soon they would be over enemy territory, and shots might be fired at them. No matter how he had heard about it from others or tried to imagine it himself, this was still flying into the unknown. He suddenly realized that this was for real, and his senses seemed to become detached.

The Halifax gave a mighty lurch upward as the pitch of the engines seemed to strain. The burst of adrenaline that this engendered brought Len's focus back while he sorted out what had happened. It came to him quickly that the skipper was just squeezing more height out of the kite by "getting up the stairs." Barry had heard about this from some of the other pilots back at RAF Rufforth, their HCU. It was a process of flying the aircraft as fast as was dared in level flight and then quickly applying some flap to urge the crate higher. It was done in successive steps and hence its description. Even though the old, clapped-out Hallies they flew during their heavy conversion training at Rufforth were loath to accede to such methods, they had practiced it on several occasions. It was only once they had tried it on the operational bombers they flew after arriving at 158 Squadron at Lissett that Barry was sold on this technique.

Barry loved altitude. His strategy for getting through his tour of thirty operational sorties was going to be based on height. Many of the other pilots also thought that this factor was critical for survival. The theory was that if you went in at the briefed altitude, Jerry already knew where to concentrate the flak and defences. Most of them chose the easier way to find this quieter air, if they dared to deviate from the mandated height, and simply fly a thousand or so feet lower. In an underpowered aircraft like the Halifax Mark II, standard issue to many Group 4 bomber squadrons, this made perfect sense. But Barry also had a preternatural phobia of ordnance hitting him from above, so if he was going to find a different place from which to do his duty, it would be higher. In any case, Barry saw all this as just another challenge to his seemingly limitless confidence. In every such contest, Len had seen this man have the skill to match.

After yet another course of apparent level flight the bomber shot upwards again, leaving Len's stomach somewhere beneath them. "Git up dem steps, Skipper!" Boots, the wireless operator shouted over the 'com. Boots always kept the crew loose, but there was a time and place for such levity.

Barry's quick and business-like response reminded their W/Op that his attention should be on the task at hand. "Wireless Operator, any updates on the winds?"

"None, Skipper," was Boots' contrite reply. The admonishing message was received. In a few more moments, yet another "step" was felt. And then another, but each passed without commentary. The increased effort to get higher had another consequence, however—they would be later than many of those in their squadron when they started their bombing run. This made

Len's vigilance in looking for enemy fighters that much more important. German night fighters feasted on stragglers.

After some time, the intercom crackled to life once again with the call that made this flight so much different, "Skipper, enemy coast ahead." It came so suddenly that Len could not tell if the report had come from Vick, the air bomber, or from the navigator, David. It mattered little. Despite all the ropey do's in training and the other multitude of ways they could have gotten the chop up to now, Len palpably felt that now they were truly putting their lives on the line. His heart beat quicker for a moment, but he was ready.

Or at least he thought he was ready. As they crossed the Dutch coast, off to the port side Len could make out, through the scattered cloud, a multitude of searchlights scanning the sky near what he guessed must be Texel Island. It was probably thirty miles away, but it still felt uncomfortably close. The enemy knew they were coming. He knew he should avoid looking into the glow with his dark-adapted vision, but it was difficult to ignore. There is always something essentially riveting about knowing now, for certain, that someone is out to kill you. That his duty was to kill them did nothing to ameliorate this anxiety.

The Halifax plodded on toward their target through the airspace of occupied Holland. Only the occasional lurches generated by the skipper's now increasingly futile attempts to gain more altitude interrupted the monotonous tumult of the four engines. You could tell even from the rear turret that this valiant aircraft was at its ceiling and could give no more height, but Barry would keep trying. *Just keep weaving to give me a view below, Barry,* thought Len as he scanned the skies, *and forget about the height!* But that passing thought was quickly dismissed and left unspoken, for he truly did trust that man to do the flying.

The chatter on the intercom now began to pick up, as they were apparently ready to enter German airspace. There were many things that were usually bandied between pilot, engineer, navigator, and wireless operator, so this gave an air of normalcy to the now more perilous environment that had, for Len, enveloped the plane. Much of it did not concern the gunners, so they silently continued their watch of the skies. The one tidbit of information that filtered through, however, was that they were now just five minutes from the target. It couldn't come soon enough.

Len continued to move his turret, straining to see anything that might pose a deadly threat. It was imperative that he carefully look beneath the bomber, for his was the only position that gave even a reasonable view of an enemy fighter stalking them from beneath or behind. But all he could see beneath them was what seemed like hundreds of yellow, orange, and red flashes. The explosions in another setting might be thought of as spectacular, but they were what resulted from the explosion of German 88mm anti-aircraft artillery—flak—capable of being fired to their altitude and above. Most, for now, seemed to be concentrated at a much lower altitude, and at once, Len was thankful for Barry's prescience in getting *G for George* up as high as he had. From where he sat, he could not imagine any aircraft flying through that barrage unscathed.

The intercom was still buzzing with the chatter of his crewmates making ready to do their duty—to bomb the docks and factories of Duisburg. They were close. The flak continued to burst beneath them—beautifully malevolent flashes—but more and more seemed to be inching closer to a coincident altitude. Len's senses were already almost overwhelmed when he felt the aircraft begin to be buffeted by "dirty" air—either the bomb doors were now open, or they were being bracketed by flak. As the acrid stench of cordite from the spent flak shell explosions assaulted his nostrils, he knew it was likely both. The Jerry guns were finding their range.

Len could feel his heart racing. He was transfixed by the flashes that seemed to envelope his perch. Repeatedly they came—some near, some far—all of them deadly. He knew, inherently, that there were no enemy fighters lurking nearby, for they would not chance being hit by friendly flak. All he could do now was wait and watch … and wish that it would soon be over. He heard Vick's call of "Bombs gone!" and expected Barry to now bank the aircraft out of the maelstrom that was threatening their precarious sanctuary. But he seemed to be flying straight and level. What was wrong? Was Barry as riveted to his station as Len was? Would they just fly on this way until a shell finally found its mark?

"Okay, photo's done, lads," came the imperturbably calm tone of their skipper as Len felt the Halifax bank steeply. "Let's go home." Of course, he had forgotten that they must wait for the photoflash that was required to prove they had carried out their operation and that might give some gen to the Intelligence Section.

The exploding flak shells did not seem to abate with their new course away from the target, but this view offered another perspective. Len could now see more weaving pencils of light that were searching for his bomber and the hundred or so other Allied bombers that had been sent there that night. Down below what had just now heaved into sight was their target, well lit by the incendiaries and explosions that every crew had unleashed. In between new flashes of explosions, he could make out what seemed to be streets made of fire interrupted by a black band that must be the Ruhr. It seemed that Bomber Command had issued this target a telling blow.

Off to the starboard quarter, down, Len saw a searchlight catch a Lancaster that immediately began to dive and weave, trying to shake its grasp, but several more shafts of brilliant light caught up and their intersections soon formed the "cone" every airman feared. Now it seemed that the entirety of the outgoing flak barrage was directed at that aircraft and the seven poor souls occupying it. It certainly meant that the probing flak that had come so close to *G-for-George* diminished in intensity, at least while there was a more certain target available. Len was at first relieved for the respite and cheered for the illuminated bomber to fly clear of its entanglement. Relief turned to guilt as he watched in fascination as the bomber disintegrated into arcs of flaming petals as a flak shell found its mark. At some bomber base in England tonight, there would be seven more empty bunks.

Len's bomber seemed to only crawl from the target as the flak intensified after the respite afforded by the concentration on the doomed Lancaster. The sharp, quick flashes still came far too frequently, but again, they seemed to all be below their height. Maybe they'd be late back to base, but Barry was certainly keeping them safe. Suddenly, maybe a few hundred yards behind his turret and a couple thousand feet below, there was another greasy explosion and arc of flaming debris. In the clear air, it looked distinctly different from any flak burst, but it appeared almost exactly like what had just happened to the coned Lancaster. Len had been warned in briefings of "scarecrow shells"—sent up by the Germans to explode with all the appearance of a flaming bomber with the explicit intent to demoralize bomber crews. If that was indeed what it was, the enemy was absolutely spot on in this display.

As they crept toward home, the defences seemed to proportionally diminish. There were now more searchlights than flashes from exploding flak—or maybe it was just the distance that had stolen away their intimate proximity. Len knew that he must again become vigilant, because they were now likely passing close to the night fighter bases in Holland. The night vision had returned to his eyes and he strained to see anything that might be a prowling enemy aircraft. Wheeling the turret from side to side, he would focus out to distance and back again. He was vaguely bothered that his sight lines to beneath the bomber were restricted. He would talk to Barry about this—maybe if he could occasionally bank the kite, it might give a better view. It wasn't worth mentioning now, when the skipper was likely more than occupied, but he'd be sure to mention it to him back at base.

Len flexed his fingers to keep the numbing cold at bay. His eyes ached from the strain and the cold—despite their protection by goggles. His oxygen mask was frozen to his cheeks. The moisture from many sources had welded the rubber and leather to his skin. The flow of oxygen was cool and fresh and stung his throat when he breathed, but it was warmer than the outside air. His heated suit could ward off most of the cold, but the least protected parts, his face and fingers, were still a challenge to keep warm. He peeked again at his watch and estimated they had almost another two hours of flying before they'd be home. They had done only one night flight that had been longer than this, and that was in training over friendly territory.

Suddenly a dark shape appeared, angling obliquely to their path. Len's heart jumped in his chest as he brought his guns to bear on the encroaching shadow. He strained to make out any detail, but the aircraft seemed to just be crabbing a couple of hundred feet below them and if it continued, it would pass harmlessly beneath them. Closer now, Len could easily make out four engines and so relaxed—it was another RAF bomber. He would report it to the skipper in case he was planning any manoeuvres that would bring the two together.

"Traffic port stern quarter down, skipper," said Rollie from the mid upper turret before Len could key his intercom switch.

"I have been watching it, Skipper, it's a Lanc," added Len, hoping to not sound like a Johnny-come-lately. "It looks like it will pass behind and below us."

"Good show, gunners, let me know if he makes any sudden moves," Barry intoned pleasantly. "Keep those eyes peeled; we are still over Holland."

The other bomber passed harmlessly in a diagonal behind them with no change at all in their flight. Len wondered if they had seen *G for George*, but since there was little forward-facing armament on RAF bombers, it was likely more important that Len had made them out to be friendly before hosing out a burst of fire from his four machine guns. There had been many aircrew killed by friendly fire from compatriots who felt it necessary to shoot first and ask questions later.

Len continued his scan of the sky, but it was late already, and it seemed that even the enemy defences had gone to bed. "North Sea in five minutes, Skipper," said David from the navigator's station. It was quickly and laconically acknowledged by Barry. Clouds had now completely obscured the ground beneath them, so Len could not guess their position save for the length of time they had been airborne. They seemed to be alone in the sky. Too many crews, however, had gone missing on their first operation for Len to now relax his surveillance of the sky.

Time dragged, but eventually Len could hear the subtle change in the pitch of the engines as Barry throttled back fractionally to descend from their lofty, safe altitude. They would coast across the North Sea to make landfall not far from their Lissett base. It was a long journey over very desolate waters, but with the thick undercast of clouds below, it was unlikely any ships would take pot-shots at them now. The threat of enemy night fighters was certainly diminished as well, for it was only a real zealot that would follow them this far from their base. Finally, Barry announced to all that they were at 10,000 feet. They all knew that this meant that they could doff their oxygen masks.

Len loosened the strap holding his mask in place and gingerly peeled it from his face. He breathed in the open air and found it rife with the scents that gave him comfort—the oil from his guns, the leather from his flying kit, and even the cordite from his spent shells. These were familiar to him, but there was one more acrid smell that seemed foreign. It must be the distinctly different compounds found in the explosives of German manufacture. Holding his leather encased forearm to his nose, he took a deep whiff of its strangely exotic scent. In addition to everything else that had been unique to tonight, this odour was what was most surprising.

As they now descended through the overcast near the English coast, Len thought to luxuriate in closing his eyes, finally to rest from the strain of the nearly six hours of use since takeoff. But what he found in the blackness there forced his eyes open immediately. He closed his eyes once more but instead of peaceful darkness, he found flash upon flash of exploding flak shells. The dim light of the turret and the non-descript mass of cloud swirling past it held more comfort than the visions that seemed etched on his retina.

The dusky fields and hedges of coastal Yorkshire were now streaming past his turret. The runway threshold zipped past and, nearly coincidentally, Len felt the main gear touch concrete, and he could make out the puff of dust and spent tire that emanated from their contact, followed shortly by a waft of burnt rubber. Len braced himself for the impact of the tail wheel beneath his turret, but as Barry had so promised, after a particularly vigorous three-point landing that had jarred Len badly, it was barely perceptible as they slowed to sub-aerial speed.

They were home. As the skipper parked the kite on the hardstand, Len set to his close-out procedures. The pounding of the last seven-plus hours on his kidneys had filled his bladder to near bursting, and he could scarcely wait to scramble from the aircraft and find a nice patch of grass upon which to relieve himself. As he crawled from his turret and gathered his parachute, he saw Rollie climbing down from his mid-upper turret perch. As they moved toward the rear access door to exit, their eyes met. Len wondered if his own eyes were as wide as Rollie's in amazement ... wonder ... terror? It was difficult to tell what he saw, for there were no words exchanged. All he knew is that they had gone through it together and they were safe again at base.

One of the ground crew was at the exit. "We to't you lads were gone for the chop! Didja stop off for tipple somewheres?"

Rollie had managed to regain an air of nonchalance. "Are we late?"

"You be the last ones, now. Ev'ryone's back," called the erk over his shoulder as he tended to the main gear.

Len and Rollie found a spot for a communal bladder voiding. While there, Len ventured a comment about the experience. "That was some flak, eh?"

Rollie just laughed and shook his head ruefully. "It sure was, Len, it surely was."

The lorry to take them to interrogation soon showed and was already carrying another crew that had arrived just before. They were an experienced cadre, and their casual banter suggested that they had had an easy time of it. The truck stopped off at the debriefing building, and the crew followed Barry's proud march to sit at the nearest unoccupied table. Barry was smiling and calmly drawing on what must have been his first post-flight cigarette. The intelligence officer asked the usual questions about the trip to the run-up, and there was little to report. It was all standard until the bombing altitude was asked.

"Twenty-two thousand feet," said Barry, matter-of-factly, but he could not help himself but to puff out his chest marginally.

The SqIntO paused in his transcription and looked levelly at their skipper, "Twenty-two! ... Are you certain of that?" Barry did not waver in his gaze at the officer. Before he could speak, the only other man who would have had firsthand knowledge of the altitude, Harry, from his flight engineer station, spoke up. "Twenty-two thousand it was, sir, and maybe just a wee bit more." The officer sighed and began writing down the offending figure for posterity while Barry simply gave a casual shrug, as if to say, any decent pilot could do that.

The interrogation turned to the accuracy of the bombing and the results. Vick reported on his targeting and release. Len finally chimed in to report that he saw the city ablaze, and he could see the glow of the fires until near the Dutch coast on their return. The intelligence officer then asked about the German defences that they had encountered. Len was about to answer when Barry cut him off.

"It was a very quiet trip, and the attack seemed to be going well as we left." The authority and coolness with which it was spoken seemed to signal to the IO that there was nothing more to be said, so he took this down verbatim. The statement, however, left both air gunners, Len and Rollie, with their mouths agape—both having seen the flak shells appearing to carpet the entire target area beneath them. They then looked at Vick who, from his bomb aimer's station might have had the best view, and he was also agog— his eyebrows threatening to rise to his hairline. Len thought, *Well, if that is the way the skipper saw it, who are we to argue?*

The crew was dismissed, and they found their way back to their quarters in short order. It had been at once a very exciting but very tiring day. Every time Len closed his eye even briefly, he could still see the multitude of flak explosions or the cascading fountain of burning wreckage from the two bombers he had witnessed go down. Barry's choice to get above it, by any means, likely made it the "quiet trip" he reported. What was cemented in Len's mind, and likely the minds of the rest of the crew, was that this pilot was one who could bring them through this. Barry's cool confidence likely didn't need Len's support, but tonight's adventure ensured that he would have it forever.

There was one last thing to do before Len settled down for the night. He took his logbook from the makeshift desk near his bunk and unsheathed his pen. Along with date, time, and flying hours to record, there was one line, about three inches wide, in which to record all the salient points of the night's duty. The RCAF clearly didn't expect its personnel to wax eloquent on their experiences! Len thought for a time before writing, "OPERATIONS: DUISBURG" and then paused slightly before adding, notwithstanding his proud skipper's assessment, "HEAVY FLAK." He closed the book and turned off the light.

7

The church was quiet save for the soft shuffle of those still returning to their seats after Holy Communion. I was kneeling, emulating my father, taking all my cues from him. I was still new at this—my First Communion, a big thing in our family and in the Catholic Church, was only a few weeks ago. We had celebrated it in grand fashion with photos taken of me in our yard, suitably dressed in spanking new white shirt and black pants. Having two older brothers from whom I normally inherited a wardrobe, this was a grand thing!

Dad turned and offered his prayer book to me, pointing with his thick fingers to a particular passage, and then tracing its length with the inferred command to read it. I took the well-thumbed, heavy volume from his hand, careful not to make any sound in the reverent silence that always pervaded this time of Mass. Dad slid back from the kneeler into our usual pew near the side door of Little Flower Church, but I sensed his eyes on me as I studied the words on the page.

> *What has passed our lips as food, O Lord, may we possess in purity of heart, that what is given to us in time, be our healing for eternity. May Your Body, O Lord, which I have eaten, and Your Blood which I have drunk, cleave to my very soul, and grant that no trace of sin be found in me, whom these pure and holy mysteries have renewed. Who live and reign, world without end. Amen. We humbly beseech You, almighty God, to grant that those whom You refresh with Your sacraments, may serve you worthily by a life well pleasing to You. Through our Lord Jesus Christ, Your Son, Who lives and reigns, world without end. Amen.*

There were many words in this prayer that were completely unfamiliar to me with the somewhat sparse vocabulary of an eight-year-old, so I understood very little of what I read. I focussed on words such as "drunk" which, I knew, had so many negative connotations. And what did "cleave" mean? "Beseech!" What a strange word, indeed! I had never heard it and had no idea how one would go about beseeching anyone or anything.

I read it again to no advantage at all. I simply held the book and stared at the word "beseech." For reasons known only to my subconscious, I envisioned a tree, and then a sandy beach, and then a vast ocean. I abruptly stopped my reverie when I felt I had attended the book long enough and I carefully handed it, still open, to my father. He closed it gently as he took it back and then smiled at me. I then watched as his eyes turned slowly to the altar as he viewed the closing Eucharistic rituals of the monsignor and altar boys. He appeared to be at peace.

Len stared at the corrugated ceiling of the Nissen hut as he lay on his bunk, his fingers interlocked behind his head. The barracks was nearly deserted with only a few colleagues puttering in the quiet mid-morning hours. He replayed last night's operation in his mind. It was only his second with his new permanent crew, but it was now the eighteenth of his tour. He felt good about these chaps, and last night's return trip to Kassel was all the proof he needed that this was a good crew.

Still, there were too many things to contemplate after the sortie they had. Every trip out it seemed offered something new—new things to see, new things to fear, new things to challenge him, new things to bring him closer to his crewmates, and new things to try his soul. As was usual, so many things seemed out of his control, and he was very familiar with that feeling. But still he mulled things over to try to make some sense from all of it.

They bombed Kassel last night, and from all accounts at debriefing, it was a good prang despite the less than auspicious beginning. The Halifax bomber that was next taking off after his had crashed on the runway. Len, in the rear turret of *J for Jane*, had a front row seat to that show. The smoke and flames were vivid reminders of just how capricious life could be flying operations in

Bomber Command. They had learned after they had returned that *P for Peter* had blown a tire during the roll just before takeoff and swung off the runway, where its undercarriage had collapsed and made a mess of one of the main runways of Lissett aerodrome. The entire crew had gotten out and escaped significant injury. They were, however, one of the few crews to occupy their own bunks overnight. Most crews were diverted to RAF Catfoss for fears that the returning crews might not be able to handle a cross-wind landing on one of Lissett's other runways.

Len smiled to himself. The gents in the control tower didn't know his new skipper, Robbie, very well if they thought something as trivial as a crosswind landing would dissuade him from returning to the comfy confines of his own barracks. They should have also known better than to think he would easily take a redirection to Catfoss. Robbie was still in the first half of his tour but had proved himself to be a much better than average pilot, and one on whom the leaders could depend. He also had the steely confidence in his own abilities that would have him unlikely to back down from any flying challenge. This was the skipper who brought his kite back from the previous trip to Kassel on just two good engines. A cross wind landing, even after a seven-hour round trip to Kassel, hardly qualified as a challenge.

Only a handful of crews landed back at base last night, and that easily explained the sparse population in quarters and at breakfast this morning. Several crews had returned early and did not carry out their duty, owing to difficult flying conditions or mechanical failure. The deep overcast last night held a significant icing hazard, but most crews would sooner "press on regardless" than to append "D.N.C.O"—Duty Not Carried Out—in their logbooks. Those flights did not count toward your tour, and most believed that if you were going to risk anything, you may as well risk it all.

Two crews did not come back last night. That in itself was not an anomaly, for it seemed that 158 Squadron would often lose ten percent of the aircraft they sent. Len now scarcely paid attention any more to the losses. In most instances, that he noticed at all was simply because it meant that it had not been he who had "Failed to Return." But one of the two crews was captained by Barry, the man with whom he was originally crewed—the man who had gotten him through months of training, who had flown so brilliantly through Len's first eight sorties and from whom Len was nearly inseparable. Essentially, his brother had not returned.

Last night's was Barry's first operational flight back with 158. He had been gone for months, hospitalized following an ill-advised sprint on Len's bicycle after a particularly spectacular night of drinking. Barry could fly a Halifax bomber like few others, but his skills were markedly less prodigious on wing-less wheels, especially after consuming copious amounts of bitter. He might have escaped the incident with only his ego bruised if he hadn't been trying to also transport even more libations in bottles secreted in his uniform trousers. The nasty lacerations required stitches and a long convalescent leave.

The incident had also meant that his crew—the six that were all still in fine fettle, if deeply hung over—were now without a skipper. They became "spare bods," free to be snapped up by other crews either temporarily or permanently. Len had flown with several others in the interim, but after holding out for three months hoping for Barry's return, it seemed they were never to be reunited. And so it was a happy coincidence that a pilot of Robbie's calibre was looking for a replacement air gunner only a few weeks ago. Len jumped at the chance.

But then Barry came back last week, pronounced fit again, and was assigned a new crew. Len was disappointed to not be flying with Barry again but was still pleased as Punch to have him back at Lissett. Almost at the same time, Barry's commission had come through, so a big piss-up was organized to celebrate the reunion and the promotion. However, on this occasion, Len had made certain to hide his bike.

And then last night's operation to Kassel. There was something about October 22. On that date two years ago, Len had enlisted. Last year, he had left Canada for England on the same date. And now this. He tried to convince himself that news would eventually filter back that Barry was captured and still alive in a POW camp. He knew it was a long shot, but with Barry's skills at the control of even a damaged aircraft, it might be true. The only other recourse was to hope that he'd been lucky. Len had seen too many instances of luck only being of the bad variety to go down that avenue.

Suddenly a loud *rat-a-tat-tat* made Len jump nearly clean of his bunk. People running a stick along the corrugated ribs on the outside of the barracks always produced this cacophony. It jangled frayed nerves and had long since ceased to be funny, so Len was ready to give whoever had done this tired gag a real blast. The door flew open and in leapt Pappy, his new crew's navigator, issuing a cackle that would have deflected even the sharpest tongue.

"Heya Len, m'boy," offered Pappy, "looks like our 'thirty-six' has come through. The crew is goin' into Brid. You are coming, no?" Robbie's entire crew had requested a thirty-six-hour leave, since it was Saturday and it seemed with all the kites trickling back from Catfoss through the day that the squadron was not going to be called on to operate tonight.

"I wouldn't miss it, Pappy!" Len forced a cheery riposte. He had planned to go into town this weekend if granted leave in any case. This would give an alternate excuse, and the company of his crew might keep him from dwelling too much on the vagaries of late October. Being with these blokes would be good tonic.

"I am going to see if I can scare up a few more spare bods," Pappy said. "I dunno when the rest will get back from Catfoss with this weather, but we may as well snag as many as we can. You gonna just be hanging around here for a while?"

"I'll check my calendar, Pappy."

"Good show, Len. We'll know where to find you." And with that, Pappy bounded out as easily as he arrived.

Len liked Pappy. Everyone, it seemed, did. He was also RCAF and a western Canadian like Len. He had joined Robbie's crew at the same time as Len, as a replacement for the original navigator who had gone inexplicably missing. The "missing" in this case was not as in the usual sense that aircrew suffered. He had simply disappeared from the squadron and then claimed some sort of temporary amnesia. He was quickly shuffled off base to other duties. It seemed a less rancorous departure than that of the man whom Len was replacing on the crew. That rear turret gunner had refused to fly just before taking off on an earlier operation and had been deemed LMF— "Lack of Moral Fibre"— and subsequently disciplined.

"Moral fibre" seemed a strange term to Len. He was uncertain if he would describe himself as having an abundance of it, but he knew for certain that he would never abandon his mates. Loyalty and duty were everything for the job he signed up for in the first instance, but even more so for the people with whom he flew. He could predict with some confidence that all in Robbie's present crew felt the same.

Pappy was a case in point. There could not be a more dissimilar personality from Len's than this wiry, garrulous raconteur. He was also a couple of years older than the rest—hence his nickname. He was known throughout the squadron for his unique character, and nothing seemed to concern him too much. He was Jewish and would tell all who would listen that with the Nazi's known attitude to his ethnicity, he would surely "end up as soap" if he was ever shot down. That he punctuated that statement with his infectious laugh only highlighted his devil-may-care manner. He was one of two commissioned officers on the crew, but as in most crews, rank meant very little amongst the guys.

The door flew open again and Pappy's obvious silhouette now had company. Len could just make out the tall, willowy kid now in tow as one of the new lads, also a Canadian, who joined 158 Squadron just a week or so ago. He had seen him around the barracks and briefings and knew that he was an air gunner like himself, but little else had been gleaned from him. Len jumped up and got his hat and coat and moved to join the two.

"I could only find one other hardy and willing soul," said Pappy. "Len, you know 'Slim' here?" The lad winced at that introduction. He stood several inches taller than Len, and actually had to extend his hand down to Len's in greeting.

"I prefer 'Bud,' Len," he said as they clasped hands. "I have seen you 'round and I am very glad to meet you." Len shook his hand firmly. He was always amicable toward his colleagues but had long ago learned to be careful about whom he got to know and like. In this precarious business, friendships were often forcibly fleeting.

"The rest of the lads are up on the main road awaiting transport," Pappy interjected. "I told them we'd meet them there."

On the walk to the main road that ran through the centre of the village of Lissett, Len learned that Bud hailed from rural Ontario and was excited to get into the fray. Len had often encountered such enthusiasm, but had usually seen it dull in equal measure after the first few operations. He found that it was best to let the sprog lads experience that for themselves.

At the junction they met the other five from Robbie's crew plus a few others that they managed to cobble together for the trip into Bridlington. To Len, the well-known resort town on the North Sea coast was always outwardly welcoming but generally unprepared for the raucous activities that usually resulted from airmen winding down after ops. That there were a few Canadians in the mix today, known as second only to Aussies for their antic exploits, usually had the locals a bit more fearful for their property and kin. Overarching this, however, was the genuine gratitude that was expressed by the locals to all the airmen—especially those volunteers from the Commonwealth who had chosen to join this fight.

The consensus on the ten-minute drive into Brid was that they'd start at the Beaconsfield and move on from there. For many wearing the RAF uniform, that pub was too close to an old church and its seeming glowering disapproval. That never bothered Len too much, as it wasn't the church of his religion. What he didn't like about the pub was that it seemed to attract a larger proportion of servicemen who were trying to cash in on their self-perceived status with the local ladies. Pickings were slim enough in that department without wading through all the would-be Lotharios spinning tales of dubious exploits.

The transport soon disgorged the party near the Spa and they headed on down the road to their first stop of the afternoon. It was quiet for a Saturday but that was not unexpected—most of the crews were still making their way back from RAF Catfoss, and it was still early in the day. Soon enough they had assembled around a couple of tables in the pub and all had a mug of foamy libation in their hands. That there were ten of them seemed, to Len, to be nominal. No doubt they would lose a few but gain a similar number throughout the night. The conversation naturally turned to the newcomer, Bud, who looked vaguely uncomfortable, as if folded into a seat that was clearly built for someone of smaller stature.

"So, Slim, are you itching to get yer first op under yer belt?" queried Paddy, the other gunner on Len's crew, in his curiously deep brogue. Len noticed Bud slightly wince at the use of that moniker. He would have to get used to it. Len was one of very few who seemed to be called by his Christian name. Most others got hung a nickname and, once attached, it was tough to shake. Paddy had long ago accepted that being from Eire, his nickname was *de facto*.

"Oh yeah!" Bud said with probably too much enthusiasm. "I just wish it would be sooner than later."

"Well, we know you been through all the training, but listen to a wee bit of gen from the ol' heads," Paddy started. "I dunno which kite you'll get, but make certain that you keep the Perspex and guns clean yourself. Don't tink the erks'll do it for ya."

"Don't be hosing out tracer until you can see what colour the Kraut's eyes are," offered Len matter-of-factly. "OTU is far too optimistic about the range of your Brownings, and you don't want to alert any other night fighters in the area." Len hadn't really learned this until well after his time at the Operational Training Unit and his first few sorties. It had only been adequately conveyed to him during the week he did at Gunnery Flight in Leconfield in July after Barry's crew had been dispersed. It was the one good thing to come from Barry's accident.

"Keep your eyes on the dark," warned Robbie. "Don't look at searchlights or fires. Keep your night vision fresh." An earnest nod was the only acknowledgement offered from the now- rapt student.

Stan, Len, and Robbie's air bomber now took up the lesson as he leaned forward as if to impart what was clearly the most important message. "If you gotta bail out, and you find that your chute doesn't open, you must, must, MUST hold your left hand high into the air, like this." Stan said with intoned gravity while demonstrating.

"Why? ... Why should I do that?" Bud had instinctively leaned in to catch this vital piece of information. Len knew what was coming next.

"In case anyone wants your wristwatch!" half the group shouted in answer before howls of laughter pealed from the table. Bud at first looked shocked and then joined the rest in their mirth. Though Len had heard it before, it never failed to bring a smile to his lips that faded only when the ale beckoned.

Many topics were hashed out and they were on their third round when Pappy elbowed Len in the ribs and motioned toward another table where two flight sergeant RAF pilots were having an animated chat with a couple of the local ladies. "Look at those two 'line shooters.'"

Len turned to see one of them gesticulating wildly with two hands, obviously pantomiming two aircraft in mortal battle. Len and Pappy rose as one and moved behind the airmen but in full view of the two lovelies at the table. They leaned in and chanted in unison.

"… there I was, upside down in a cloud, on fire, with nothing on the clock but the maker's name!" It was the standard, practised riposte to any airman caught "shooting a line." There was nothing more disgraceful than to be caught exaggerating your own exploits with other air crew within earshot—no matter what the potential libidinous reward. The two pilots fell silent and at first looked ready to fight, but then their shoulders slumped as they glanced at each other sheepishly.

Len wasn't sure if the response could be traced to the pilots being caught out or if the clearly Canadian accent forestalled any physical response. Canadians were renowned across the country for their size and muscularity—not to mention their often-ample pugilistic skills. Len smiled at the ladies, and both he and Pappy dipped their heads to them in parting before making their way back to their table.

It was soon Len's turn at the tap and while he tried to catch the barkeep's attention, he noticed one of the two ladies from the other table had gone to make use of the facilities. She was short but well-proportioned, and her bare calves drew Len's attention before her nicely coifed blonde hair did. He watched appreciatively as she walked from view. His distraction caused the barman to have to give him a poke to get his attention. He put in the order and slapped his money on the bar. While he waited, the lady making her way back to her table walked directly toward Len. He caught her eye and smiled in greeting.

"I fancied the way you handled those two earlier," she said, giving her head a fractional tilt toward the trio still sitting. "I swear that I have 'eard the same tale scores of times!" She rolled her eyes.

"It never stops them from trying," he replied. "My name is Len."

"Very pleased to meet you, Len," she said as she smiled broadly. "Mine's Sylvia." She reached out and touched the "CANADA" flash on the shoulder of his tunic. "You are a long way from home. How is Yorkshire treating you?"

Many dark or ironic responses reeled in Len's mind before he replied, "It's a bit damper than what I am used to, but everything has been just wizard."

"Good to 'ear. It is the least we can do." Sylvia didn't seem to be in a hurry to get back to her table as they chit-chatted, so when the pints in Len's order arrived, he thought he would make a bold suggestion.

"If you are not tied to those line-shooters at your table, do you fancy a little walk outside to get some air?" he asked, hoping to sound as unthreatening as possible.

"Just a walk?" she asked suspiciously, but her smile suggested the playfulness behind the query.

Len held his hands up in surrender, "Just a walk! These close spaces make me twitchy."

"Awright. I'll get me coat."

Len gathered the pints that he had paid for and, after spilling only a modicum, delivered them back to his mates. The alacrity with which they took their drinks suggested that they'd been growing impatient.

"Thought you'd never get away from that blonde job!" Hale, the crew's W/Op said.

"Look who's talking!" Len said as he flipped Hale's longer-than-regulation blond locks. "Besides, I think you ought to show more respect to my future Missus!" This brought hoots and catcalls from those assembled. Len just grabbed his coat and gestured toward the pint he had delivered for himself. "Give that a good home if I am not back in an hour. Cheers!"

Sylvia had likely taken a similar length of time to extricate herself from her companions, because she arrived at the door at the same time as Len. In deference to the eyes that followed them out, she waited until they were on the street before she took hold of his proffered crooked elbow. They walked slowly toward the beach, just a block or so from the pub.

Evening had almost set, but there was still sufficient light to clearly discern the vast expanse of the North Sea spreading out before them. This view of the ocean was strangely comforting to Len, who had grown up thousands of miles from any such water. It was likely that it was reminiscent of the waving fields of grass or grain crops at home, but the constant crash of the surf was foreign. Sylvia's gentle but firm grip on his arm made him almost forget where he was and his far from certain future. The two stopped, arms still entwined, short of the barricades—far short of the barbed wire and anti-invasion defenses on the beach.

"I always loved this spot when growing up here," said Sylvia, finally breaking the silence that had pervaded since they left the pub. "I miss being able to run on the beach. I can't wait for this to all be over."

Len never allowed himself to think that far into the future. He didn't like to contemplate the many ways in which "it all being over" could be connoted. "The sea looks a lot different when you are flying over it," he said simply, not mentioning the terror that he felt whenever he mulled over a ditching in its icy black waters.

The warm softness at his side and the sweet scent of perfume encouraged Len turn to his companion and look into her deep, inviting eyes. He leaned in as her eyes closed and her lips softened. They more closely embraced as their lips found each other's. The sensuous nature of this moment was in such sharp contrast to everything Len had experienced in the last twenty-four hours that emotions seemed to evade him. Although he tried to summon the passion, for there certainly was shared attraction, there was no spark. Sylvia clearly sensed this, and their lips parted but their embrace lingered.

After some time, they fell back against the fence over which they had been viewing the sea and looked back down the lane toward the nearby church and the pub where they had met. Their entwined fingers were all that was left of the aborted tryst. The long silence was broken by Sylvia. "I learned how to tell time from the clock in that church's steeple."

"My church back in Canada didn't have a clock or a steeple," said Len, and he realized too late just how quickly that would kill the conversation. Their moment was now gone. Like so many other things during this war, it was sudden and fleeting. They wordlessly started a slow stroll back up to the pub and their waiting friends. Len savoured the dependent soft clutch on his right arm, but he wondered when he would allow someone to be there more permanently. There seemed little point in starting anything when his certainty seemed to exist only to the next op, if to then.

They rounded the corner at the pub to find a knot of blue greatcoats loitering in front. It was Len's mates. Sylvia saw them and, in acquiescence, stretched up to give Len a peck on the cheek while whispering a parting, "Thank you," before scooting back through the door. Len walked sheepishly back toward the group, not knowing what reaction awaited him. He had only officially joined this crew a few weeks ago, and although they seemed to have fully accepted him, he still felt a little like an outsider.

"Took care o' that pint like you said, mate," Lofty, Robbie's long-time flight engineer, said as he patted his midsection as if to confirm its deployment. He was several inches shorter than most in the crew so came by his ironic moniker quite honestly. Len was likely not a lot taller than he but was stoutly built and easily had two stone over his slight but wiry crewmate. He stood naturally at Robbie's right shoulder like he was meant to be there and would never leave. Len had never consciously noticed that before, but it seemed entirely natural.

"We're heading over to the Brunswick now," said Robbie with the quiet authority that always seemed to fill his voice. "Are you done here?"

Len was relieved that that was all that was said about his brief time with Sylvia, and he welcomed the discreet consideration. "Yup, we can head on over."

It was quite a few blocks to the Brunswick Hotel, but it had long been the favourite watering hole for the established Lissett crews. It was small but welcoming. It also had the advantage of being one of the pubs closest to the rail station, which served those who would travel that way—often making the short hop from the Burton Agnus station, the nearest rail stop to RAF Lissett, or RAF Driffield, 158 Squadron's former home. More importantly for Len, it was much closer to where he wanted to be when the night was over. Still, it was a fair hike through most of downtown Bridlington from where they had started, but the cool of the evening air might refresh them for what was proving to be a long night of socializing.

Len looked forward to the stroll. He was fascinated by the age and character of the buildings. Nothing in his hometown of Lampman dated back more than forty years. His grandparents had been amongst the earliest set-tlers and were founders of schools and commercial enterprises. Bridlington was by no means a town of antiquity, but almost everything here was so much more established than at home. It was completely foreign but still strangely attractive.

The Brunswick was getting busy by the time they arrived. Several of the crews that had been diverted to RAF Catfoss had now found their way into Bridlington. There promised to be more whispered discussions about last night's operation to Kassel in the next few hours. They were tasked to not talk about it, but some details always found their way out. Of course, Len was most interested if there was any more news of Barry. But that was unlikely. Most of the operational crews now in attendance were replacements for those who had gone missing in the three months since he was away, medically grounded. Still, he needed to try.

The mixing and mingling in the pub was in full swing now, but a crew still tended to stick together. Len was happy for this insulation from the other crews this night, for his thoughts were elsewhere. Your mates on the squad-ron never asked you about your mood, even if you appeared introspective. The most you would ever expect was an encouragement to "have another." In their shared experience, they had all had ups and downs. Camaraderie is what sustained them.

Despite the convivial cheer that surrounded him, Len knew that the longer he stayed, the more difficult it would be to fulfil the mission he had set himself this weekend. He had not really paid attention to what the others had planned for the remainder of their pass. Closing time would soon come and "last orders" would be called. This often did not mean that the evening's fes-tivities would be at an end—the local constabulary would often turn a blind eye to the legalities of the situation, and "drinking-up-time" was less often a rule than a guideline. Still, Len wanted no part of any of it. He needed to leave.

He made a show out of looking at his wristwatch and announced simply, "Well, chaps, I'm off."

"Ahhh … I knew it!" chirped Pappy, as he nudged Len in the ribs. "You're in with that blonde bint from the Beaconsfield. I figured you were just plottin' the course earlier, you silly bugger." Several of the others hooted or chimed in with suggestions of varying degrees of lasciviousness.

Len said nothing in response, but the blush that accrued from the graphic talk clearly left the appropriate impression with his companions, for none urged him to stay. Indeed, they seemed to be encouraging his hasty departure as if in vicarious relish. He quickly gathered his coat and accoutrements and simply waved his friend adieu and, exiting into the cool, late evening air, turned up Manor Street.

Len walked slowly. He was in no rush. The solitude was welcome after the high energy of the evening. It certainly gave him time to recharge. He often wondered if his preference for the rear turret on operations reflected this in his personality. He was very happy to be part of the crew, the team, but he also appreciated being on his own. He paused to peer into the window of one of the many shops that dotted this part of the old Bridlington Town.

The street was murky as he travelled away from the few bits of stray light that escaped from the Brunswick Hotel. Britain was at war and the blackout was near total, especially with the moon still yet to rise this night. That didn't bother the man whose life often depended on how well he could discern things in the dark—his eyes were like a cat's in this environment.

The shops gave way to residences as he left the commercial district, and the street curved away in response. Len followed but made a sharp left turn and paused, stood in front of a building that was largely indistinct from the surrounding brick edifices in the neighbourhood, aside from the two steeples that reached into the night sky and its heavy oaken and iron front door. He ambled solemnly up the short walk into Our Lady and St Peter Catholic Church.

The heavy door swung open with some effort. Len was thankful that the same restrictions to opening that concerned pubs did not apply to churches. As he expected, the church was empty. The light from several votive candles provided ample if flicking light in the narthex as Len walked the short distance to the stoup, unbuttoning his coat as he went. He dipped his hand reverently into the holy water and crossed himself before genuflecting and kneeling in one of the trailing pews. He looked toward the large crucifix behind the altar, and a flood of memories of Sundays past reeled in his mind.

Although this was not his home parish, the canonical structure gave famil-
iarity, and the many hours he had spent in devotional attendance seemed to
mesh with this present one. He had struck this same pose—knelt with fingers
intertwined—for Sunday Mass, weddings, and funerals back home. The
sorrow of the joint funeral mass for his father and brother was only barely
eclipsed by the faith that he and his family had done all they could to deliver
them to the Lord's hands. And now, he would pray for all the people he had
lost more recently. So many! Some were those whose faces he could scarcely
recall; others were closer than brothers. He would offer a rosary for each. It
would be a long night, but it was the very least he could do. He withdrew the
simple string of beads from an inside pocket, kissed its attached crucifix, and
began his devotions.

Hours passed as he scarcely moved except for the reverent fingering of the
beads in his hands. Light in the church changed subtly as candles expired
and then as the moon rose higher after midnight, its light pouring through
the high windows. The repetition and meditation brought a calm over Len
that he had not felt in months. He was solitary in this church through the
night, but he did not feel alone. Only last night, he was by himself in the rear
turret of a heavy bomber but felt his six crewmates, their intimate presence
engendering a similar reliance. In either setting, the future was largely out of
his control. Another chaplet soothed past his lips and digits.

The Church would always be an integral part of his life. Len's mother, as
so many devout Catholics do, hoped that he was the one in the family to
follow Holy Orders. The tacit pressure to enter the priesthood seemed only
in abeyance when he joined the RCAF. But everything Len had experienced
since joining the fray had militated against that. All the things that he had
seen and done in the past two years were in clear opposition to that path.

He could still feel the warmth and smell the scent lingering from his brief
liaison with Sylvia. It distracted him from his devotions even now. A wife?
A family? A future? So many times, he had convinced himself that he would
not see tomorrow whilst on operations that he scarcely ever believed anymore
that he would. Maybe if he ever got out of this, he would find someone with
whom to build a family. Though he might not survive, certainly a family had
a future. The next rosary would be offered to his future—his family.

It was only when dawn's light started to creep in through the east panes that Len realized his vigil had been through the night. It was what he had planned, but he had never expected it to pass so quickly. His paramount need to find what washroom facilities the church offered topped his seeming urgent need for a cigarette. He would look after both in short order.

Outside the church he found a nearby alley in which he could lean against a high fence and enjoy a few of the Canadian cigarettes he had saved for occasions such as leave. The calming draws of smoke seemed to punctuate a return to the mood that he had forged before the events of the last couple of days. It would be okay now. He would stick around for Sunday morning Mass and then get back to base.

Len saw a uniform striding past the head of the lane and recognized its occupant immediately.

"Hey, Fitz!" called Len. The figure stopped abruptly and turned. Fitz was another RCAF gunner at 158 Squadron. He was from a small town in Alberta and one of few other Catholics on base. Their origin and religion bound them if few other things did. They had found their way to services here one or two times. Fitz, not unexpectedly, stuck with his own crew with these few exceptions.

"Lenny, my boy!" said Fitz with a wide grin of recognition. "Have you been here long?"

"Just got here," Len lied. "When did you guys get back?" Fitz's crew was one of the many that had accepted orders to divert to RAF Catfoss on their return from last night's target. Len pulled out his package of Sweet Caps from a pocket and shook one out with a practiced flick of his wrist to offer his comrade. It was accepted with a nod.

"Late afternoon yesterday," said Fitz. "The weather was ghastly all day. How'd you manage to land back at Lissett?"

"Just lucky, I guess," said Len. "Is everyone back?" Len still hoped against hope that Barry had shown up eventually.

"Still the two FTR." replied Fitz. Using the acronym didn't soften it any when you already knew that they had "Failed to Return."

"Did you see the huge bang when we were on the way back?" Len said, changing the subject to avoid having to dwell on the now-apparent loss of Barry and his crew, not to mention the other seven men whom he barely knew. "It looked like half the city blew up!"

"Yeah! We were fifty miles past already when she went up," Fitz said in amazement. "I wonder what the hell that was!"

"I dunno. We were even farther out," said Len, not caring for the King's Orders against discussing operations this one time. "Whatever it was, Jerry deserved that and more …" He trailed off, but his vehemence hung in the air, as both stared silently up the alley.

A carillon from another distant church stirred the peace of this crisp Sunday morning, calling to its members that services would soon start. "Time to go in?" Fitz asked finally, gesturing to the parishioners trailing toward their church. Len nodded in assent as they twisted toes simultaneously on their discarded cigarette butts and fell into step as they moved toward the church.

8

The house was surprisingly quiet. There was usually at least a muted din in our small abode with our family of eight crammed into such small quarters, but things had gotten considerably more tranquil as of late with my eldest brother moving out to an apartment of his own, leaving only two boys to share our room. This June Saturday found my father and I each reading quietly in the otherwise abandoned living room. I was sat cross-legged, engrossed in reading my favourite volume of the *World Book Encyclopedia*. My father had extravagantly purchased this set a couple of years back. Dad was ensconced in his easy chair, poring over another extravagance—the most recent weekly edition of *Time Magazine*.

We had not had a lot of treats growing up. I am certain it was not easy to raise a family of six children—especially when a goodly portion of Dad's paycheque went to his attempt to tithe the Church. But things were recently turning around for him. His work as a health inspector for the city was now starting to garner the financial remuneration that it deserved. As well, Mom was working part time on weekends, which helped financially, now that the family was maturing and needing less constant nurturing. To top it off, my brother moving out had further lessened the familial financial burden. The prized set of encyclopaedias, given a plum place in our living room bookcase, was a prime example of what we might now afford. It was entirely within my father's character that he would try to give his children an informational advantage with whatever disposable income he might have. His own perk was understated—a subscription to a newsmagazine, something I also read cover to cover when he was finished.

"Holy cow!" Dad suddenly exclaimed, giving me a bit of a start in the quiet of the afternoon. My head jerked up from my glossy-page tome to regard him. My father seldom swore, and for him to attach "Holy" to anything was noteworthy. "Son, come look at this!" he said, waving the magazine.

I carefully closed the volume, set it down, and rushed over to where he sat. The page was open to several black and white photographs showing the result of Israeli air strikes on Egyptian Air Force targets during what was to become known as the Six-Day War. The images were aerial reconnaissance of aircraft parked on runways or surrounded by revetments. All were heavily damaged—some were still smoking. Images of war were commonplace in 1967, as it seemed the world was spiralling into chaos, so I was not overly impressed by this new portfolio.

"Now that is what I call precision bombing!" Dad continued, pointing at a photo of three aircraft neatly destroyed on their hardstands. Such photos were in all media, so I really didn't see what the fuss was about. I simply nodded in acknowledgement and then went back to my reading. Volume "S" of the encyclopedia included my favourite topic of "Space Travel." Pictures of burned out airplanes could not match diagrams and descriptions of space-craft and the narrative of the history of rocketry and its pioneers, the likes of Goddard, Tsiolkovsky, and von Braun!

Len waited on a hard, wooden chair outside the flight commander's office. The summons to speak to the flight commander, a squadron leader by rank, had come just after breakfast, and Len made certain not to dawdle. The "Skew-ell," a New Zealander, was a likeable fellow—laid back as most of his countrymen were, but you did not achieve such a rank in Bomber Command without having paid your dues, and part of that was observing the required discipline. Len had primarily observed him from a distance, where his informal manner was quite refreshing in the often-aristocratic military hierarchy of the RAF. Still, it was always easier to step down from rigid for-mality than to try to approach it from the reverse. He unconsciously stiffened his seated posture.

He was not told what the subject of this meeting would be, but Len could well guess. He had not been detailed for operations in almost eight weeks. Yes, there was a considerable time spent on a well-deserved leave after the grind of his first eight operations on Barry's crew. But when Barry went "non-effective" following his accident, Len was hoping against hope that he would be still re-united with his friend and skipper. Most of the rest of the now-headless crew had already flown operations on other crews or had chosen to join them permanently. Len had forestalled such a course of action by volunteering for further training at Gunnery Flight, RAF Leconfield. Len sensed that the latitude he had been granted in waiting for his friend's recovery had worn thin.

It wasn't that he was trying to shirk his duty or that he refused to fight. It was not that at all. He only felt that making a switch before all other alternatives were explored was akin to desertion. He had too much invested in his prior crew to make such a change so capriciously.

The door to the office rattled suddenly. A sergeant pilot that Len had seen before but could not put a name to stepped out smartly and left the door open in his wake. "He'll see you now," he said as he walked briskly down the hall to the building entrance.

Len stood quickly, straightened his tunic, and marched into the flight commander's office as smartly as he could. He fired off a crisp salute and stood at attention before the officer, who absently returned the gesture while shuffling some papers on his desk.

"Close the door, Sergeant, and stand easy," said the officer in the somewhat distinctive twang of what Len knew to be a Kiwi accent. Len always fancied the New Zealand dialect to be a muted blend of Australian and English. It had neither the unpolished edges of the former nor the often-posh surliness of the latter. Many could not distinguish the difference between the speech of the two races of colonials from down under, but to Len it was as distinctive as the Canadian's from the Yank's.

"A couple of things, Sergeant. I haven't talked to you for a while, so I thought I would catch up," the commander started amiably. It was little wonder the man was so popular with his charges. He had a way of putting you at ease with just his manner. He had already flown a full tour. He clearly knew the men needed no more stress in their lives.

Len simply stood waiting for what was to come—encouragement or admonishment—it was difficult to tell from how this had started. He was already feeling some guilt about not having been on ops, but he did not want to say anything to elicit a dressing down.

"How was your time at Leconfield?" asked the flight commander.

"Very good, sir!" Len answered with what he hoped was the appropriate amount of enthusiasm. "I was surprised how much more that there was to learn after training and ops." He had spent just over a week with the Gunnery Flight boffins, honing his craft. They had flown in the *Defiant*, an aborted interceptor equipped with a Bolton Paul gun turret. He had also gotten to know the long-since abandoned two-engine bomber, the *Whitley*. Almost the only things still serviceable in those aircraft were the guns.

He suddenly realized that this meeting today might be due to the Leconfield instructors seeing fit to put in his record that he had augmented his training by shooting up a nearby flock of seagulls. He had then used those rapier skills to deftly sever the tow cable of a practice drogue with a somewhat unlucky if uncanny aim on a subsequent flight. Both had caused some consternation but were not that far out of the realm of usual hijinks for airmen. He hoped the incidents had not followed him back to his home base here in Lissett.

"By all accounts, your time was very effectively spent," the superior officer said with what Len could detect was a slight smirk. "You should be a great asset to any crew here."

Oh no, Len thought to himself, *here it comes. I am going to be assigned to another crew.*

"It doesn't look like your skipper will be back any time soon, and most of your crew have already taken spots in other kites," the officer said. "We can look for a permanent posting for you or we can keep you as a spare bod."

Len was discouraged by the news that Barry's convalescence was going to be longer than anticipated, but was thankful for the opportunity to take his chances that they might still fly together again.

"I am happy helping out whoever needs me, sir. They are all good chaps," Len said, hoping that this would not sound like faint praise. He would wait for Barry while flying with all and sundry. He thought it worth the risk.

"As you wish, Sergeant," the squadron leader said evenly. "You'll be on the battle order as a spare gunner. Looks like you might go tonight. Ops are on and it seems we have a few of your mates out on sick call."

Len was not surprised by this. He was somewhat relieved to be back in action. There had been some guilty pangs every time he heard the heavies starting up to go out while he sat in the sergeants' mess or at his bunk.

Len was about to give his dismissal salute when the officer glanced up at him one more time and said, "Oh, and stop by stores. You ought to sew on your 'Crowns' before briefing. Your promotion to WO2 came through this morning. Hop to it, Mister, and congratulations."

The newly minted warrant officer stood stock still, stunned by this news. He had been expecting the worst at this meeting, and he was going to be walking out of it up a rank. He somehow saluted and croaked out a "thank you" to the grinning man behind the desk before bolting from the office. He looked down at his sleeve where he would soon sew on his new rank insignia—an understated embroidered gold crown. It was going to be a good day.

That afternoon, Len was just finishing the tailoring that his promotion required when Tom, an RAF pilot and rather recent addition to "A" Flight, came strolling past his bunk. He stopped as Len was admiring his handiwork.

"Keen!" said Tom, gesturing to the new addition to Len's tunic sleeve. "Congratulations, Len. I guess you'll be buying in the mess tomorrow." Tom had only been posted in to Lissett less than three weeks ago but had already been racking up operations at such a rate that most considered him a seasoned pilot.

"Thanks, Tom!" Len replied. Although the RAF air crew often complained that the colonial air forces seemed to earn their promotions much more quickly than those in the English branch, most of the kudos that Len had received today seemed genuine. So it was with Tom. Len liked him. He did not know him too well, but their shared quarters and assignment to 158 Squadron's "A" Flight had them at least on a first name basis.

"Len?" Tom started, "I saw your name on the flight list of spares today, and my arse-end has got some dread pox or something today. I thought you'd come with us tonight."

"Sure thing, Tom," Len said. "When is the general briefing?"

"We'll swing by sixteen-forty," Tom replied. "Seems we are to report to briefing as a crew and stay together throughout, so it's easiest if we go as a group."

This was somewhat unusual. In Len's experience, the main briefing was always a bit more informal than what Tom intimated. Perhaps this was the new squadron commander putting his own stamp on things. This was the first week under the new commanding officer—the previous one having failed to return on ops to Nuremburg just seven nights ago. It was always appreciated by the members of the Squadron to have a CO that put himself on the top of the battle order, but it was always a sobering blow when someone of that high station and extensive experience went missing.

Tom's all-RAF crew, sergeants all, came to collect Len at the appointed time. Although as a Canadian he often felt out of place in this English dominated squadron, he had one further thing to set him apart today—his rank. Although he was certainly proud, he did not want to have it negatively affect the way the others viewed him. He hoped that this crew would accept it as a sign that he was at least an experienced and competent replacement for their usual rear gunner.

At the briefing it was soon clear that this session was different. If the Service Police checking identification at the door wasn't enough evidence of that, then the preponderance of their ilk ringing the perimeter of the room was. Len had been to a dozen briefings and never had he seen the likes of this. Yes, there was usually some suggestion of security, but at most it was provided by one or two SPs, who often seemed to just be marking time. If this was solely due to a new squadron commander, his wasn't going to be a fun tenure.

The briefing started precisely at 1700 hours with the station brass and section heads striding to the slightly raised stage at the front of the room where a curtain covered the details of the planned operation. The CO, his braids denoting the rank of wing commander still fresh on his sleeve, waved to his minions an order to pull back the drapes.

"Tonight's target is Peenemünde," he said simply.

There was a murmur throughout the room that Len could easily interpret as a collective expression of "What the …?" for it was on his lips as well. They had become accustomed to the many different names of targets throughout the Reich, and those in the Ruhr Valley or Berlin itself always drew groans or expletives. Given the unique environment in which this briefing had started, it was appropriate that the target was one that seemed to confound.

The map revealed a long ribbon stretched out across the North Sea and then angling through Denmark to a spot on the northern Baltic Sea coast of Germany. A hundred miles to the south was Berlin. At least they were not going to "The Big City" tonight with an unfamiliar crew, thought Len. Thank heavens for that! The next thing out of the CO's mouth, however, put paid to that small mercy.

"This target must be destroyed. If you do not accomplish that tonight, you will be going back tomorrow, and then the day after until the job is done." He paused for effect, but few in the room had ever heard such an edict. Any target on German soil was going to be a difficult trip. The same one on subsequent nights removed any conjecture for enemy defences and would undoubtedly result in a shaky do, at best.

The CO continued with the details of the raid. It was a mixture of good and bad news. It seemed that 4 Group of Bomber Command, of which 158 Squadron was a member, would be in the first waves of the attack. They might catch the enemy unawares—before enemy fighters could suss out the bomber's target. They were, however, directed to attack from low altitudes— from lower than 9,000 feet! They might be sitting ducks for even lighter flak batteries. They had better be in the first waves if they were going in that low.

"One more thing," the CO said with no hint of levity. "If someone reveals this target to anyone outside this room, I have been assured that they will be shot." The silence in the room was such that you could easily hear the squeak of the man's shoes as he left the stage.

The station commander then took the dais. Usually of less operational stature than the squadron CO, the man in charge of the station was often less a pilot than an administrator. If he spoke at briefings, it was usually just some cheery bucking up. But as an experienced RAF man, noticeably older than the previous speaker, he likely recognized the anxiety of the audience.

"No worries, lads. Intel promises that the target is lightly defended. Recon showed, at best, four catapults." This was met with a smattering of nervous laughter from the assembled crews. "We have also been assured of a spoof attack on the Big City by *Mossies* of PFF complete with T.I.s and route flares." The Path Finder Force usually led the way on attacks with Mosquitoes dropping route markers for the main force and then denoting an aiming point with Target Indicators. Such a diversion, if successful, would buy invaluable time for the initial waves of the attack by drawing enemy fighters from the actual objective.

The general briefing continued with meteorological and other sundry logistical information being conveyed—most of which Len did not need. It did, however, return the atmosphere to one of almost operational normalcy and ease—if such a thing could exist for a group of young men about to fly into mayhem. Finally, the CO took centre stage once more and dismissed the squadron with a cheery, "See you in the smoke!"

Len sat quietly with Tom's crew, of which he was an integral part tonight. He knew this trip would be different, and its importance was highlighted in any number of ways by the briefing but no less than by the wingco's promise to be at the head of tonight's battle order. He could only imagine what was going through the others' minds at this moment, but their silence intimated that his anxiety was shared. The euphoria that accompanied the news of his promotion had been replaced with the same familiar knot in his gut that accompanied flying, even with familiar crewmates. Finally, Dennis, the air bomber of the crew, broke the silence.

"Lucky you found a wizzo tail end for us tonight, Tom," he said, pointing at the newly stitched rank insignia on Len's sleeve. "Sounds like we might need him!"

The amicable laughter as they rose to leave the assembly eased Len's mood. They were scheduled to be in the air between 2100 and 2130 tonight, so there wasn't much time to get all their necessary chores and preparation completed. The busy work necessary to get underway left little time to stew about what might be ahead.

In no time it seemed, Len found himself being buffeted in the familiar noisy, drafty abode of an unfamiliar rear gun turret of a Mark II Halifax—this time, it was *F for Freddie*—climbing out in the waning light of this August evening. This was another RAF crew's usual ride but now was Len's for this trip. *Freddie's* tail end, Len knew, was usually occupied by another Freddie—a happy-go-lucky cockney who had, along with his crewmates, managed to score two weeks leave after their first month on ops. The turret seemed in good order—well maintained after just a few sorties, and with a few adjustments, Len was as comfortable as one could be in the cramped working space.

Len noted differences in Tom's piloting already. He had flown with quite a few different pilots in training and air tests. Some were smoother than others. Some pilots seemed to fly as if it was second nature, while others seemed to fly like a nervous old lady driving down a narrow street. Tom seemed to be between these extremes. There is no doubt he would get even better in time. He was not Barry's match by any stretch, but he certainly gave no cause for concern. Not that Len could do anything about it at this juncture.

The bomber strained to reach their usual cruising height of near 20,000 feet. Len felt the icy chill of the air as it tried to invade creases and crevasses of his flying suit. Just a brief time ago he was sweltering in the still warm late summer evening on the taxiways at RAF Lissett, and now the biting chill of the upper atmosphere made that a distant memory. They had climbed through the promised broken mid-level cloud and were now over Denmark. Soon they would make a starboard turn and hoped they'd look, to all the enemy defenses, as part of a stream of malevolence headed for the German capital.

The plan, as they were briefed, was to maintain their usual height until nearer the target when, over the Baltic Sea, they would dive down to under 10,000 feet to attack. If Len listened closely enough to the banter between the skipper and navigator, or if he carefully applied what he learned in the briefing, he would know that they were getting close. But all he needed was what he felt in the seat of his pants. He had felt the long slow turn. He had heard the pitch of the engines change as they rapidly descended, and, moreover, he had felt the subtle changes in gravity as the aircraft neared Peenemünde.

Len also felt the buffet of the turbulent air disturbed by scores of other bombers flying through this small area above the target. It was always a worry that you might collide with one of the hundreds of others sent to rain destruction here. They were low now. Len could make out whitecaps on the sea surface below as he did his programmed search of the sky for enemy fighters, but the environment was remarkably free of defences of any kind—fighters, searchlights, or flak. He would not be lulled, however, and he strained his eyes to detect any sign that they might be stalked.

Over the vibration and noise Len could hear the instructions Dennis was feeding Tom from the opposite end of the Hallie. Out the back, all Len could see was the blackness of the sky and the subtle shifts of dark tone behind them that delimited the sea from the land. The sky seemed to be lightening from ahead of them as Len felt the extra drag that open bomb doors created, and the slight increase in power that the skipper applied to keep the aircraft level. The intercom crackled.

"Bomb on greens, Dennis. Bomb on greens," announced the wireless operator. At first it seemed strange that the W/Op would be interrupting at this point, but then Len remembered that there was some arcane talk at the briefing about them employing a "Master Bomber" on this operation, and that the crews should listen to instructions over the wireless. It all made this operation that much more surreal to be going in so low, taking orders from someone in another kite, over a target he'd never heard of.

Now Dennis' voice was all he heard through his earpieces, and he strained to peer through the diffuse glow that now seemed to be overtaking the bomber. "Okay, Skipper … steady … steady … right … steady. Green T.I. in the sight. Steady … steady …" To Len, this process seemed to take forever, but perhaps being away from operational flying for two months had warped his perception of time. Finally, he heard the familiar call: "Bombs gone!"

F for Freddie was carrying only incendiary bombs tonight. Len had asked during boarding so that he would know what to look for on the ground as they overflew. Their bomb bay was filled with canisters of hundreds of small, thin, thermite-filled, square magnesium tubes designed strictly to start fire on whatever they struck. The earlier waves of bombers had almost exclusively carried high explosive bombs that would rip apart wooden structures. Now, the incendiaries would hopefully destroy by fire what had been rent asunder by the preceding HE.

As they held steady for the target photography, Len saw clearly how low they were. He also could not take his eyes off the shockwaves of high explosives and the white-hot magnesium fires that were taking hold of the rows of apartment-style living quarters below. His mind harkened back to briefing where they had been told, for the first time in his recollection, that their objective this time was to cause loss of life. They all knew that that was what likely happened when they loosed their ordnance on what to this point was usually described as targets that manufactured the German war machine. Today, they were trying to kill. In viewing what was unfolding behind and beneath his perch, they were accomplishing that task. Len had never seen such destruction.

He knew he should still be scanning the skies for fighters, but his night vision, so carefully preserved through the flight so far, was irrevocably spoiled by the brightness of the fires just a few thousand feet below. They were now turning sharply for their trip home. There were a few light flak batteries pumping their usual malevolent strings of "flaming onions," but they seemed uncoordinated and somewhat random. There also seemed to be some hint of a smoke screen starting over the target area that might be set to hamper later bombers. Or it might be just the result of the countless fires that had started to take hold. He looked for any sign of enemy fighters but found none.

Soon they were clear of the immediate target area and starting their slow climb back to normal cruising altitude. From Len's perspective, they were once again heading north, for he could sense ocean beneath them once more, and the glow of the fires in the target area, still pestering his peripheral vision, was nearly dead astern. Tom, in the pilot's seat, started to give the aircraft an occasional waggle to help his gunners peer as well as they possibly could beneath their bomber. This was always done by good operational pilots. Flying straight and level was a sure way to be opened up, can opener style, from beneath by a stealthily approaching enemy fighter. RAF bombers had no belly turrets. He wasn't as smooth as Barry in his waggle, and a bit too predictable in timing, but Len took advantage of every opportunity to crane to see beneath *F for Freddie*. There was still no sign of trouble.

After some time, Len heard the navigator give the skipper a course change to fly west again, as planned, and he felt the aircraft bank to port. Soon the blackness of the Baltic Sea was replaced by the blackness of land. Only the slightest shift of tonal variation revealed the change in landscape below, but the night vision had returned to Len's eyes. But every time he scanned the vista to his right he saw the glow of Peenemünde, despite them having left the area nearly forty minutes ago. They must be more than a hundred miles away by now! Len considered remarking on this to his crewmates, but he was worried about being too chatty with an unfamiliar crew. Certainly a few others on board would also have noticed, but no-one else had said a word.

On yet another scan of the area beneath the aircraft, Len thought he saw a flash, and his heart skipped. Was a fighter about to attack? He checked the area where he saw the light and forced his eyes into focus, as he had trained, from near to infinity and back again. He saw it again. It was on the ground and quite distinct: three short flashes, a longer one, and then a long pause. Then it repeated. It was Morse code for the letter "V." Len had retained that much from the courses at Initial Training School. "V for Victory." Some gallant Dane on the ground below was risking retribution from occupying forces to signal his support for the bombers droning overhead. A couple of minutes passed and there was another flash from the ground—the same message but not quite as polished a delivery. Len smiled to himself and keyed his intercom connection.

"Skipper, from rear gunner, 'V for Victory' from the folks below," he reported with some pride.

Almost immediately, Dennis chimed in from his view at the opposite end of the Halifax, "I have seen a few too, Skipper!" They would be just as obvious to the air bomber through the clear Perspex at his position.

"Very good, lads," said Tom, but added facetiously, "Did you want to fire off a Very cartridge in reply?" The message was clear. There was still work to be done before they were home safe, and they ought to concentrate on that. Failing that, they may as well announce to everyone where they were.

Thus, suitably chastised, Len continued his scan of the sky, but their increasing distance from the target made enemy action increasingly long odds. He did see a few more lights from friendly occupied folks below, but made certain to keep it to himself. No matter what, the reassurance that they had support from the people under Nazi oppression made him feel that what they were doing was worthwhile. The obvious results he had seen leaving Peenemunde was confirmation. The drafty and isolated rear turret from which he did his duty didn't feel quite as cold and lonely this night.

It was shortly after 0400 when *F for Freddie* touched down back at RAF Lissett. Although he should be tired after such an eventful day, Len's nervous energy left him almost ecstatic. He hurried through his post landing chores but made certain to leave everything just as he had found it. This had been his first trip as a replacement, and he didn't want to step on any toes with any crew that he would be more than happy to fly with again. The regular gunner would find the turret in tip-top shape.

The crew was all smiles as they met under the aircraft, and already there was good-natured banter between them and with the ground crew who were now fussing over the aircraft. The lorry would soon be here to take them for the ritual of interrogation. Tonight, it seemed that no one had any reason to dread the pointed questions from the "spies" in the Intelligence Section. It had been a text-book operation.

As they boarded the transport, to a man, they lit up celebratory cigarettes. They talked in excited, staccato bursts. There seemed to general agreement. They would not need to go back again tomorrow, but such a determination was to be made at a level far above Len's recent promotion.

"We really got 'em tonight, eh?" Len said to the group and then turned to Dennis and added, "I bet you put those sticks right in Jerry's pickle barrel."

"It was a good show." Dennis deflected any untoward praise. "The Master Bomber was spot on with his directions. It was a nice prang."

"Wizard prang!" Tom re-affirmed, using the most recent common vernacular, just as the truck lurched to a stop outside the debriefing hut.

Len liked the sound of that. Short and sweet but described his day perfectly. He already knew what he'd write in his logbook for tonight. It had been a good day.

9

"How fast can you drink that?" Dad asked as he motioned at my nearly-full glass of water. We sat kitty-corner from each other at our kitchen chrome set. The bare skin exposed by my short pants stuck fast against the new plastic that covered the somewhat inexpertly reupholstered chairs. He wore long pants. I never saw him in anything but long pants.

"Pretty fast!" I quickly replied. I had worked up quite a thirst helping him with yard work on this warm summer evening. I don't know how much assistance my puny arms could have rendered, but Dad always had us helping out when there was work to be done. He had cut the grass with our manual rotary mower, and I had helped rake and gather the clippings as best I could. He had filled up two glasses with ice-cold water once we had finished and re-entered our house.

"Show me." He gestured with his nearly full green aluminum tumbler toward mine.

I leaned to the task, drawing several deep gulps and swallowing as rapidly as I could. Some of the water sloshed past the widely out-turned rim and dribbled down my chin and onto my t-shirt. I heard my father laugh as I drained the glass and wiped the spillage with the back of my hand as I had seen so many actors do in television westerns, and I heaved a triumphant sigh.

"Good job, Son!" I smiled at that. Nothing feels quite as warm as a father's praise. But he soon added, "Watch this."

He tilted his head back and opened his mouth. At the same time, he seemed to grasp his throat on either side with thumb and forefinger. I thought I heard a slight anatomical click as he seemed to swallow against the pressure of his digits. He took the full glass that he was holding and simply poured its contents into his mouth and apparently down his throat without any hint of pause or, for that matter, spillage. As he finished he looked at me, and a broad grin filled his face—no doubt my astonishment was amusing—as he ceremoniously turned his glass upside down on the table.

I was speechless as he explained, "We used to do that with big glasses of beer during the war." He held his hands up and down, about a yard apart, to indicate the size of the glass containing the beer. I could not even begin to comprehend. That could not have been Dad! There was nary a beer to be seen in our household, ever.

"I even won a contest," he said with a wink. "I will show you how when you are older."

How could this kind, caring, and gentle, if often hopelessly clumsy man (it was he who had ostensibly "redone" our kitchen chairs) be the same as the one who would, or could, drain a yard of ale? It seemed utterly incongruous to me. How else could he surprise me?

Len peered out into the early January damp drizzle that seemed entirely appropriate on this morning. Yes, it was intermittent and not nearly as beastly as was often the case in what passed for winter here on the North Sea coast of Yorkshire. But this was where the powers that be had found enough flat land to construct RAF Lissett, so here he was stationed. This was now his second winter in England, and 1944 was shaping up to be no better than the first. It was just dismal. But today, he would have wanted it no other way.

The posting in the sergeants' mess this morning, that Len always ruefully scanned, had brought the worst news of his entire RCAF experience. It was conveyed in the tidy, officious language used in Air Ministry issuances—the list of those attached to 158 Squadron about whom news had been garnered. In it the missing, captured, and dead always read like morning roll. With some of those named, you had shared a pint or a cuppa, while with others you could scarcely attach a face. Today's reading felt like a kick in the gut. Barry was dead.

News trickled out of the German-occupied continent at no certain pace. Sometimes it was only weeks and news of the loss of an entire bomber crew was confirmed, while more often, the requisite six months would pass without substantiation before the fate could be made official—presumed KIA, Killed in Action. That was always the case for the poor sods that went down in the North Sea without a trace. Or for those lost in the innumerable flashes euphemistically termed "scarecrow shells," where an entire bomber would be blown to pieces so small there wouldn't be any sense in collecting them. Well, thought Len, there must have been enough left of his dearest friend to at least identify. Barry had failed to return in late October.

This was not a surprise to Len. Other members of his original crew were gone now, too. Boots was the first to go missing in August. Most of the crew that that happy-go-lucky wireless operator had joined were reported captured that night, but Boots and another were still missing. There was always a chance that he was evading and being sheltered by the underground, but it was a strange thing—you always seemed to sense when there was hope and when there ought to be none. Perhaps it was the closeness that formed with each crew, but Len knew, despite his best efforts to keep the man's spirit alive in his heart, that he was gone.

And then Rollie went for the chop in October. There was no word of his fate either, but his entire new crew had failed to return—a crew in which Len had once flown as replacement—once more scanning the skies with his friend and fellow gunner. Yes, Len's crew had only picked up Rollie when they had started in on Hallies at the Heavy Conversion Unit, but the bond formed between the only true defenders of the aircraft was the closest to teamwork that air gunners on heavy bombers often felt. Out of all the crew, it was Rollie who had best honed Len's drinking skills. It was impossible for Len to think of that irrepressible bloke without a smile tugging at his cheeks.

It seemed that losing friends and colleagues was what this war was all about. You woke up each day—sometimes exhausted from operations, sometimes still tainted from the pints you put down the night before—but always still alive. It was always the other guy who "went for a Burton." It was that simple belief that kept you going. But Barry! Dead? The man who had gotten Len through so many scrapes, operational and otherwise, and whose piloting skills seemed as if he was always destined to fly, was gone. It seemed to

change everything, for now doubt gnawed at the fringes of his blissful ignorance—or moral fibre. (Those two qualities, it seemed to him, were easily
interchanged.) If Barry's exceptional abilities had not staved off his seemingly
capricious demise, then what might happen to the crew of the only man Len
might grudgingly admit was Barry's equal, if not superior, in piloting skills.

As if on cue, Len recognised the casual if confident gait of his current
skipper strolling across the compound to the barracks. Although in his RAF
greatcoat Robbie looked like any of the hundreds of other NCOs at the base,
his particular amble, hands thrust deeply into pockets, was unmistakable to
Len. Or perhaps it was his rather prominent ears seeming stuck on, as an
afterthought, to the sides of his long face. The man exuded competence and
inspired confidence. Len's mood brightened, if only fractionally.

Robbie smiled warmly at Len as he passed him at the entrance of the
Nissen hut. Len would never reveal any hint of the arc his thoughts had taken
during what must have been the several minutes he had been staring out into
the grey morning. He welcomed the likely change of topic into something less
introspective and sombre, so he returned the grin as best as he could muster.

"Just having a chat with 'Flight' and a few of the chaps," said Robbie as
he unbuttoned his heavy coat. "No flying for us today. A few crews are being
detailed for local flying, but we are off the hook."

"It's just as well, Skipper," Len said, shaking his head. "I wouldn't send a
dog out on a day like this!"

"You're not made of sugar, are you?" came the quick retort, but with the
sparkle in Robbie's eyes Len knew this was just the usual teasing. "I reckon
you would rather be shovelling snow at -40 back home in Canada?"

"In a heartbeat, Skip, in a heartbeat!" said Len. "That's why I love it at
20,000 feet. I am in my element!" They both laughed at that. Len imagined
his stories of winters back home in Saskatchewan were wearing thin on those
who still listened to him.

"The brass hats still haven't got everything sorted out with the new kites,
and there seems to be more gen coming down the pipe all the time," Robbie
continued in a somewhat more serious tone. In the last few weeks the squadron had taken delivery of over twenty new Halifax bombers. The new Mark III
version had redesigned tail control surfaces and different engines. The old

Merlins of the Mark II Halifax that they had been flying were replaced with more powerful radial engines. All the crews had been getting acquainted with flying the new aircraft—practice bombing, cross-country flights, and fighter affiliation. They seemed a very worthwhile upgrade in terms of speed and ceiling, but to Len, his turret looked almost exactly the same.

"It looks like we are losing "'C' Flight" to a new squadron based at Leconfield. They will fly from here for the time being until the transfer is worked out." Each squadron was sectioned into smaller divisions termed "flights." Robbie's crew was in "'B' Flight." All this mattered little to Len—as long it wasn't he who had to pull up stakes and move. He had some friends in "C" Flight, but they'd have plenty of opportunity to get together whenever they decided to head south to The Quaker House in Skipsea, or maybe hit the pubs in Beverly, nearer to the new squadron's home. Len knew of a few good spots in that burg from his time at Gunnery Flight previously based there.

There was a bit of a lull in the conversation, but Robbie started to laugh and then shook his head fractionally. Len cast a quizzical glance at his friend and skipper that all but begged for elaboration. Robbie complied. "The Skew-ell finished up by saying that they also had to find someone to send to Pathfinders. I thought for a minute he was going to ask us to go, but then he looked at me seriously and said, 'Who do you want to get rid of?'" Robbie laughed again, and Len guffawed in response.

The Pathfinder Force was the bee's knees according Bomber Command Headquarters at High Wycombe. They were supposedly elite squadrons that went ahead of the main RAF bomber force to mark the target so that the subsequent kites would hit the objective with greater precision. The theory was fine, but precision did not always equal greater accuracy or effectiveness—especially if the marking was wide of the intended target. PFF was sold to crews as being tough and demanding, but the truth was that flying in early often meant you faced fewer challenges getting in and out. Someone up the line recognized that for their tour was longer. Yet they still had plenty of volunteers. Maybe they attracted more skirts.

Len didn't begrudge the difficult job that many of the Pathfinders had—marking the target at low level or circling the target to direct later waves. Those guys had guts. But most bomber crews wanted to be carrying ordnance that did harm—not flares and markers. It was amusing to Len that the best way to rid your own squadron of a problem was to "promote" them. It was likely always that way. In King Arthur's day, some hotshot apprentice artisan was likely sent by his master on to the royal court, just to get him out from under foot.

When the laughter died down, Robbie started casting about the barracks. "Have you seen the lads? Since there's nothing happening today, I was thinking we might head into town to quaff a few. Are you up for it?"

"Count me in, Skipper," Len said in quick response, pushing his earlier sombre thoughts to the back of his mind. "I saw Paddy on his way to the canteen earlier, and Hale breezed through not long after. I am certain they'd all be easy to find." Len got up to get on his winter kit.

"Relax, Len …" Robbie waved him off. "I am still dressed. I will go on the hunt. We'll stop by to pick you up before we go find the bus. If any of 'em show up here, shackle 'em to a table until we get back. Cheers." With that he ventured out into the damp that you could almost see.

Len watched after him, and he could not fight the pang of guilt for the loyalty he felt to Robbie after knowing him for just a few months. The feeling was sharper today, now that he had learned of the demise of the man who had inspired the same in him. What did it all mean? Was this loyalty only the natural outgrowth of the being a "crew"? He knew from the many conversations he had had with colleagues and acquaintances that such fealty was not automatic. That some would do almost anything to rid their crews of a sub-par crewmate or even pilot. Pappy, their recently acquired navigator, was originally crewed with a pilot who routinely lost consciousness on every flight above 10,000 feet. It was a wonder that it took them nine ops together before they approached the Skew-ell with their concerns, and they were subsequently dispersed as spare bods while the pilot was shuffled off to other duties. Yet with others, loyalty to each other was clearly unbounded— the crew carrying a weaker member that might even lead to them getting the chop because of purposely overlooked incompetence. It was a difficult dynamic to figure and, for Len, this day of all was the least likely in which he'd suss it all out.

He thought instead of the experiences he'd had with Robbie and his crew. It was the usual mixture of duty and decompression; tedium and terror. Len had gone on seven ops with this slender man from Lincolnshire at the controls, and they had completed six of those duties. The seventh was a supposed "milk run" to Cannes during which the port outer engine on their venerable old Halifax Mk II, *Jane,* inherited from another crew that had completed their tour, decided to go unserviceable as they crossed the French coast at Le Havre. Len had been wary of so called "pieces of cake" ever since his harrowing return from Le Creusot, when Barry had nearly run them out of petrol. This time, the engine didn't just pack up, but it threw the kite into a spin. Having the aircraft swap ends was not a sensation nor view Len appreciated, but Robbie's superior skill brought it under control after a few revolutions and a screaming dive. There was just no way to "press on, regardless" that night, because the recalcitrant engine would just not feather, so they were forced to turn back.

All of it, of course, was funny now, and much good-natured abuse was heaped on the skipper for his impromptu aerobatics. Len didn't escape blame either, for Paddy decided that the reason they all got a panoramic view was because the man in the back was bored with his rear-only perspective. It turned into a perfectly serendipitous crew-bonding exercise when they were forced to land away from base at RAF Hurn. Pappy, always the biggest character on the crew, wove some of his usual double-talk, wrangling, and intimate knowledge of the King's Orders (and all its loopholes) into a windfall payment from the station accounts clerk to each of the crew for their stay in the area. Len still shook his head at the revelry that resulted while they waited several days for the repair of their aircraft, for he, too, had played an integral role in their hijinks.

The crew was always looking for dupes they could challenge into "putting down a yard." It was a typical wager you could find in most English pubs. Who could quaff the two or so pints of ale contained in the traditional long, tapered, bulb-ended glass in the shortest time? Many establishments had a pair of these glasses reserved for such bacchanalian tilts, and those pubs were always favoured by Robbie's crew—but only when they had their "ringer" in tow. Len learned of his "talent" quite innocently. Rollie had taught him the basics in any number of drinking holes around York when they joined up while riding out their conversion to heavies at RAF Rufforth. But Len had far outpaced his mentor when it was discovered that he could suppress the swallowing mechanism and simply pour the libation down his gullet. Rollie's tutelage helped him master "the swirl"—a necessary skill to aid the beer funnelling down the narrow shaft of the yard glass at the optimum rate.

Their enforced sojourn in the Bournemouth area when they landed at Hurn provided several opportunities for challenges to be made in new venues. The wagers were often enhanced when the crew would trot out their rather unassuming Canadian air gunner as their champion. Len was happy to do it—even if it meant that an activity that was initially undertaken to relieve stress had now almost taken on the pressure of operations to "Happy Valley." But he knew that it was far from being his only valued duty in the crew.

The sudden opening of the barracks door broke Len's reverie about those nights. He recognized the tall, slim man as the seemingly permanent "spare bod" RCAF air gunner who was inexplicably still waiting for his first operational flight despite having been posted in over two months ago. He was good company and often tagged along with Len and his crew.

"Heya, Bud!" said Len in friendly greeting. "Whaddya know for certain?"

"Same shit, different pile, Len," came the quick retort. "You?"

"Same here," Len said with a smile and fractional shake of his head. "Robbie's off trying to round up a crew for a trip into town. I reckon you're welcome if you want to hitch up."

"I might just do that. There ain't zip going on around here," Bud said. "Do you think there will be many going?"

"Robbie says there's only a few detailed for flying today, so I imagine there could be a fair few," Len said in reply, but could not tell from Bud's non-verbal reaction if that would persuade or discourage.

Bud carried on to his bunk area and puttered a few minutes before returning, apparently all ready for the pilgrimage.

"Say, Len ..." Bud started uncertainly, "I heard that you went to the skipper's parents' place while I was away at Driffield last month."

It seemed presumptuous of Bud to be calling Robbie what was normally only used about one's own pilot. Len had no idea where this might be going, but it was no secret that Len had joined up with Robbie at his home during leave last month. He would answer honestly. "Yeah, I did," Len acknowledged. "The entire family is wizard. Did you hear that his folks cooked up a rabbit so tasty that I could have sworn it was chicken?"

They both laughed deeply at that. Len cast his mind back. It was a very relaxing few days with home cooking and hospitality. Although it is always difficult to forget the country was at war, the time away from Lissett was much appreciated. There was even the luxury of a visit to the local cinema, where they had a devil of a time convincing the attendant that Len's crown rank insignia on his sleeve still meant that he was an NCO. Officers had to pay their way in while the non-commissioned ranks got in for free.

Bud turned serious. "Do you think the skipper could put in a word with the brass to get me on ops sometime soon?" Bud intoned. "I am almost thinking of getting fitted for a white feather!"

"Bull!" spat Len. "There haven't been many ops to speak of in the last month. Don't forget we just got the new kites." But Len understood all too well the man's feelings of how his paucity of operational experience might be perceived. "Robbie won't mind if you bend his ear. I am not certain if he has a lot of pull with the muckety-mucks, but tryin' never hurt anything." Len knew that Robbie's opinions carried weight with his superiors, but he didn't want to give this sprog gunner too much hope.

That seemed to ease Bud's mind some, so they sat making chit-chat until it appeared that Robbie had assembled quite a crew to go on down to wait for the local transit to take them to whatever destination they fancied that afternoon. Generally, it did not matter where they ended up—certainly not to Len—but some had favourite spots, and some had ulterior motives for proximity to certain amenities. Len tried to not ask too many questions about such activities.

The bus ride was as Len anticipated. Far too many personnel with nothing to do on this dreary January day were clamouring to board the bus at each of their stops along the way. The poor junior conductor, a not unattractive lass who looked no more than eighteen, was trying to cope with the multitude of male passengers, some of whom, having sensed her neophyte status from her easily flustered manner, were determined to make her life more difficult.

It always fascinated Len that some men just never grew out of dipping a girl's pigtails in the inkwell as the best way to curry favour with the opposite sex. None of it was unnecessarily crude or obnoxious and some of the cheek seemed, to Len, quite clever. He enjoyed the interplay without participating. In due course, the young lady's superior boarded the bus. He was clearly a man not fit for national service, yet he wore his transit uniform as if he had just been mentioned in the *London Gazette*. He began to quiz his minion about the progress she had made in sorting out all the passengers, and when she admitted that she had barely started, he started to harangue her mercilessly.

"Hey Gov," said Hale, Robbie's fair-haired W/Op as he waved an interrupting hand in the portly man's direction. "Leave the bird alone. She's wizzo amongst this lot."

The agent stiffened to his full, self-important height and turned to confront the man who had dared to intercede. "I am the conductor here. Do not interrupt when I am performing my duty, or I shall have you off this trolley!"

Len watched in bemused fascination. He knew these men so well he could easily predict how this would play out.

"Aye," replied Hale, "and just how do you reckon you'll manage that?" He set his square jaw defiantly. Len had heard this tone in Hale's voice before. The usually jocular man was not to be trifled with when his back was up.

The conductor looked at Hale, but what suddenly seemed to dawn on him was that the bus was filled with blue uniforms, the clear majority of those belonging to stout men who were now murmuring in agreement with Hale. Len, too, issued a somewhat simian grunt of assent from his closed mouth. The man knew enough to cut his losses. He quietly moved to the exit and was gone at the next stop.

The jovial atmosphere soon returned after the brief, tense interlude. The bus continued its way through the smaller satellite compounds and villages surrounding the air base, but trended steadily to Bridlington. It was clear there was not much on for the day, as there seemed to be no shortage of soldiers, mainly RAF, flagging the vehicle down at nearly every stop. By the time they reached The Spa in "Brid," the passengers were fair hanging off every corner of the transport. They barely waited for it to lurch to a stop before they started to pour out—some scattering haphazardly while others were forming in more comfortably-sized groups before setting off.

The group that consisted primarily of Robbie's crew started to amble northeast as if by rote. The Brunswick was less than ten minutes away—five if you were thirsty. The boys, seemingly without discussion, had decided where they would end up. It was all okay with Len. Although he revelled in the camaraderie that seemed natural to this crew and their hangers-on, some of the solace that the beers had once brought to his often-frayed nerves had been muted as his days on squadron piled up. There were times you just could not drink enough to dilute some of the stark experience. Today, Len felt, was one of those times. Although the sky was starting to clear, the damp cold persisted. He had decided that that would be the focus of his misery today—he had successfully pushed the rest of what troubled him to the recesses of his mind. He tightened the collar of his greatcoat.

"Why the hell doesn't it just snow and be done with it?" Len said suddenly. "This damn place doesn't even know how to have winter!"

The others just burst out laughing. They had heard it all before. Paddy was first up, "Snow drifts whiter 'n thicker dan a clood!" he intoned with his lilting Irish accent. More laughter. Then Lofty, "Ey, 'n colder than 20,000 feet in January!"

But Pappy, born and raised in Calgary, quickly came to the defense of his western Canadian comrade. "Ahhh, you buggers wouldn't last a week back home, right Len?" Bud, still trailing the crew, chimed in in affirmation.

Len was just silent as the laughter and catcalls died away, but he appreciated the ribbing just as much as the support from his countrymen. There was no better feeling than to be in a crew.

As the group turned onto Bridge Street, they spotted a knot of men in uniforms that were not the standard blue of which they were all too familiar. There were several infantry and artillery regiments from the British Army whose bases were in the Bridlington area. These were obviously some of those out on their own reconnaissance. It was clear that they were heading in the same direction, and there was little doubt as to their destination. Although there was always mutual respect between the branches, there was similar pride in one's own and the natural rivalry born of it. Robbie's crew never fought with them—they simply practised their own form of one-upmanship. One that Len's hidden talents ensured that they would always win.

"Well, lads, it looks like drinks are on the brown jobs today," Robbie intoned as he surveyed the army men disappear into the Brunswick.

The wheels in Pappy's head were already turning on how to work this one. "Len, m'boy," he said as they all turned their eyes from their destination to their trusted air gunner. Pappy clapped a paternal arm around his shoulder. "Are you thirsty?"

Len said nothing at first but smiled inwardly; anything for the crew: *this* crew. "*Once more unto the breech, dear friends, once more…*"

10

The exhaust fumes from the family's Mercury Meteor hung in the air over the lane behind our house. Dad had left the house fifteen minutes earlier but had re-entered several times because of some trouble he seemed to be having. I stood on my tiptoes on the cold, bare tile floor, still in my pyjamas, to peer out the "girls' bedroom" window to see what the commotion was on this frigid winter morning. Indeed, most of the family had assembled around this one window—Mother included. The fuss had awaked all of us with several cross words being spoken as he exited the house to get back to the unfolding situation.

He, of course, needed to park the car in the back yard where he had strung an old electrical extension cord through a notch he had cut in the storm window. The electricity was to power the engine block heater in the car—the only way a car would reliably start in the depth of another Saskatchewan winter. The vehicle was now at a discordant angle across the alley, halfway into the vacant half-lot backing our yard. From the scene it was becoming clear what had happened.

In his usual desperate attempt to avoid the wooden utility pole behind our rear driveway, Dad had swung too far behind it. The recent heavy snows had obscured the wooden sidewalk that was ubiquitous in the newly developed areas of our city where pouring proper cement walks had not yet caught up with the urban sprawl. Dad had backed into the low, wooden structure and obviously holed the gasoline tank, for there was a noticeable puddle of the volatile liquid growing larger by the minute at the rear of the car.

I could just barely see Dad's hat pass beneath the window. I saw that his wide, squat frame was trussed up in his overcoat as he neared the scene. He turned at the very fence post where a gate should have hung. He had constructed the fence himself, but not being especially handy, it was devoid of the usual finishing touches. Indeed, that very post was centrepiece in a family legend. During construction, when it came time to drive the wooden four-by-four post into the augured hole with a sledge hammer, he had inexplicably chosen a wheelbarrow to mount as his perch. When his dubiously aimed blow whiffed, the result was a tribute to every slapstick routine imagined, yet remarkably yielded no serious personal injury. None in the family could see our father at that fence without the attendant story coming to mind.

Dad stopped for a moment in the driveway. Like most of his generation, he had smoked cigarettes through his youth, but I only knew him to puff on a pipe—likely under orders from his doctor. He always had trouble keeping it lit, and this morning his agitated state likely required some soothing tobacco smoke filling his mouth, so it was this task I assumed gave him this pause. Now clenching the lit pipe in his teeth, he approached the car and the widening puddle of gasoline that effused from it and then bent his head to survey the damage, in apparent ignorance of the volatile combination.

"Leonard!" My mother's shriek nearly pierced my eardrums. She started pounding on the window so hard I thought it might break, while still screaming a staccato stream of warnings and invectives. At some length, Dad either heard or otherwise sensed her desperate intervention. He stood slowly and looked back at her and gave a slow smile. He would be as fine today after this mishap as he had been countless times in the past. It was enough to make one believe in guardian angels.

Len surveyed what he could take in from the gun turret of the aged, smelly aircraft that had just recently coughed to life under him. The fuselage of the *Fairey Battle* shook with recalcitrance as today's captain, P/O Hamblyn, coaxed the single Merlin engine to life. Hunkered on the floor at his feet was LAC Richard, another member of his air gunnery training course. Len had won the coin toss to be first up on this training flight, so it was his colleague who suffered most from the pungent mélange of oil, gasoline, glycol, and spent cordite. The odour in Len's nostrils was only slightly ameliorated by the fierce blast that the now idling propeller stirred in its wake.

"Richie" was glum when the nickel that he had flipped into the air once again came up tails as Len had predicted it would. Deferential in victory, Len simply shrugged and muttered that it just must be his turn. But he was rapidly earning the moniker, "Lucky Len." It seemed he was on a streak of fortune that started with his decision to take up the air gunner trade. At every turn, things just seemed to work out in his favour since he had decided to abandon his dreams of being an RCAF pilot. Or had he been washed out of flight school? It hardly mattered anymore—things had been coming up roses ever since he became a gunner, so Len chose to remember it in a more favourable light.

This was the trainee's second hop with P/O Hamblyn this morning. Their first trip had ended up as being declared "Incomplete" due to mechanical problems with the aged aircraft that they had been detailed to use. The pilot had managed to coax it into the air, but repeated problems with oil pressure and fuel mixture meant that they were unable to rendezvous with their appointed target. Earlier, it had been a perfect morning for flying and gunnery practice, clear and calm—CAVU, as the pilots described it—Ceiling and Visibility Unlimited. Now Len's survey of the sky revealed that the warmth of this mid-July day was building numerous clouds.

The aircraft seemed rougher than usual as the engine warmed while Hamblyn ran through his pre-flight checks. In well-practised rote, the two ground personnel moved to the tail of the airplane and pitched over the horizontal surface, for a moment presenting their rumps as far too tempting targets to Len—the man with a Vickers "K" machine gun at his disposal! Fortunately, Len had seen this strange pantomime many times before. The ground crew's ballast on the tail was necessary lest the *Battle* pitch over onto its nose when the pilot ran up the engine up for its magneto check. Lucky, too, for the poor maintenance crew was that the gunnery trainees were not to engage their live ammunition until airborne. But then, all things considered, a slingshot at this distance would have been most effective.

The *Fairey Battle* had entered service as a light bomber with the RAF a scant five years ago, but its tiny bomb load and relatively low speed had quickly rendered it obsolete as anything but a training aircraft. Since it had a working, rear-facing Vickers gun in an open cockpit behind the pilot, it was well suited to the role to which it now was relegated here at the RCAF's No. 9 Bombing and Gunnery School in Mont Joli, Quebec. Len loved the flying that they were doing. The exhilaration of the speed, the sensations, and the view were at least a match for all he imagined it would be. The pilots and instructors here at the school seemed less than enamoured with their situation and equipment, but since he did not know any better, Len felt certain that he was already at the pinnacle of aviation technology.

Len felt a tug on his pant leg. Richie, crouched on the floor, cradling his own ring of shells, and waiting his turn at the gun turret. He could probably see very little past Len's flying suit save for a bit of blue sky on this wonderfully pleasant July morning. The time must just be crawling for him down below. Len bent as much as he could to hear what Richie wanted to shout at him.

"How's it going up there, Len?" he shouted over the throb of the engine and staccato rhythm of the prop cutting the air.

"Nearly ready to go," Len bellowed back. "Hang on!"

The *Fairey Battle* had no intercom, so any communication was difficult. Indeed, the pilot would only signal his trainee crew that it was safe to begin the gunnery exercise through sounding of a horn that normally served as warning to the pilot that he had not deployed the landing gear. The only other pertinent signal was a waggle of the wings that told the students that either their turn was up, or the exercise was over. Of course, there was no way for the lowly trainees to signal back to the pilot!

Soon they were taxiing, and the motion seemed to bring some calm to Ritchie's restless fidgeting. Len surveyed the scene outside his position. The treed but largely rolling landscape passed slowly as P/O Hamblyn made his way to the downwind end of the runway. The vista that looked so strange to Len upon his arrival at Mont Joli just over a week ago now seemed almost familiar. The base was still new, having only been opened a few months earlier and part of the ramping up of training for all manner of British

Commonwealth aircrew. Remnants of the trees hastily shorn for construction of the runways still littered the area buffering the taxiways. There were many changes for both the countryside and its inhabitants in 1942—especially for those literally flying through their training.

On the ground, Len found the scenery quite boring. It would likely always be that way now that he had seen how it looked from the air. The transformation in dimension and perspective was amazing, and although this was only his thirteenth flight, he was certain he would never tire of the shift in view from nadir to zenith. Hamblyn soon had the *Battle* hurtling down the runway, and the now familiar backward view that Len enjoyed changed rapidly from blurred lush green trees and shrubs to a slowly receding mosaic of forest and scattered cleared fields. The runway at Mont Joli largely paralleled the widening St. Lawrence River, less than a mile away. But from the ground you never saw the river—not like this. Now its shimmering and sparkling deep blue caught the morning sun and threw the solid, vegetated earth into sharp relief. Fair weather cumulus clouds already dotted the skies, their reflective brilliance a sharp contrast to the deep colours below. It was just before 1100 hours, late morning, but already there was some variation to the size and vertical extent of the clouds. Each one was different, but nonetheless beautiful. Len had always loved clouds, but this new perspective made him realize how much his ground-based observation had been lacking.

Suddenly, the brightness of the mid-morning was shrouded in impenetrable fog. They had flown into a cloud! The one drawback of this rearward vantage was that you seldom had any presage that this abrupt change was coming, and it never failed to give Len an awestruck start. He wondered if he would ever get used to it. Although he was largely robbed of any visibility while surrounded by the diffuse whiteness, the updraft that fed this building cloud lifted the aircraft beneath its occupants. Len's knees almost buckled as he was suddenly subjected to this new force, but he recovered quite quickly, pushing himself back upright.

The cover of the cloud gave Len time to reconnect with the purpose of today's training. As soon as they exited the cloud, Len would begin searching for the drogue being towed by another aircraft. The target drogue was a long fabric sleeve that trailed a safe distance behind a paired aircraft for the exercise. The target would be manoeuvred, often haphazardly, into positions above or in some fashion abeam of the firing aircraft. The sixty shells that filled the Vickers ammunition drum that Len clutched at his side were painted blue. Those in Richie's were red. The exercise would be scored by counting the number of red or blue stains that the bullets made in the nylon drogue. It was a challenge to achieve a high score. A successful outcome often depended on the skills of the pilots in both the gunnery and target aircraft, the weather condition, and, of course, the aspects that the apprentice gunner could himself control—his eyesight, judgement, and skill. There was some scuttlebutt on the station that for a modest sum, the otherwise meagrely paid ground personnel counting the holes could be convinced to find a few more of a particular colour. Len's ethics, however, would never permit such a thing. He had yet to score very highly on his own, but he was determined to increase his count through dedicated work and preparation alone.

Just as suddenly as they had entered the cloud, the brilliant sunshine was back. Len squinted against the sudden increase in luminance—it was not only the direct sun but its light reflecting off the nearly perfectly white cloud from which they had just exited. It was just another challenge to fight through as he blinked, tried to fight the tears streaming from his goggled eyes, and began to pivot in search of the target aircraft and its drogue.

Unbeknownst to Len at this moment was that cumulus clouds on summer days are but indicative of alternating pockets of rising and subsiding air. Now a few hundred yards after leaving the cloud, the training airplane entered a region of rapidly descending air that pushed the *Battle* downward, throwing everything in the aircraft upward. Len felt the sudden change in gravity and was immediately thankful for the safety tether that was clipped from his flying kit to the secure ring on the fuselage of the aircraft. However, with sudden panic, Len saw the tether flailing uselessly unattached at his side as his feet left the floor of the gunnery cockpit. In all his preoccupation to be ready for today's hop and his abject fascination with sightseeing, he had forgotten to secure his lifeline and now realized that there was precious little between him and the murky water of the St, Lawrence River below.

Len's left hand was filled with the ammunition drum, and training had drilled into him that he was to never lose this cargo under threat of serious reprimand. It was funny how the gunnery instructors never mentioned the possibility of being faced with the choice of dropping the drum or being flung out of the aircraft. And so training stubbornly kicked in and he clutched his ammunition even tighter. Instead he reached his right arm for anything that might save him. He was able to crook his elbow under the butt of the machine gun and held on tightly, waiting for the familiar pull of gravity to return his feet to their proper place on the fuselage floor.

Gravity seemed a long time in returning, but Len still felt secure despite his rather precarious attitude, half in and half out of the airplane, with the Vickers gun clenched firmly between his right forearm and bicep. He abruptly realized that that was not all that was holding him fast. Yes, the safety tether was still mocking him by flapping without purpose, but he felt for the first time the strong grip of LAC Richard's arms around his ankles. No doubt Richie had noticed his dire situation and lunged to keep his lucky compatriot bound to the gunner's cockpit. Soon calm returned to the air surrounding the aircraft, but not, however, to the demeanour of the two young men in the back of the *Fairey Battle*.

As soon as Len's feet were able to return to the relative solid perch of the floor of the gunnery cockpit, he quickly found his safety strap and snapped it to its securing ring on the fuselage. It is unlikely he would ever neglect to do that again. While Hamblyn flew on, seemingly unaware of the commotion behind him, Len searched the confines at his feet to try to express his thanks to Richie. When their wide eyes met, he could make out but not hear Richie's mouthed exclamation, "What the hell? ..." Len could take no time to try to explain, but hoped his appreciation was conveyed as his mouth fell open and he just fractionally shook his head in response. Richie had earned himself at least free beer tonight, if not Len's eternal gratitude.

Out of the corner of his eye, Len noticed another aircraft to the starboard beam and slightly above with its target drogue trailing behind. With the exercise imminent, Len clipped the ammunition drum to the Vickers and began training the gun on the drogue. Hamblyn started to bank and ascend slowly to intercept. The climb dumped enough airspeed that the target-towing Battle, flying level, easily pulled ahead of Len's craft, bringing the training quarry into range. At briefing today, the trainees were told that this now being their second week of training, they would be faced with increasingly difficult gunnery tasks to perform. As of yet, they had not begun any of their more challenging deflection firing—where targets approached at differing angles relative to the gun platform. Len knew from Initial Training School that his math skills were weak, so classroom exercises were not a great reflection of his abilities to master deflection shooting. It was here, in practical exercises, that he knew he must perform well or he would never achieve his goal of being aircrew. Len followed the drogue intently and mapped out at each moment where he might need to fire to hit the rapidly shifting target.

Above the bumble of the engine and fierce wind blast, Len heard Hamblyn sound the warning horn. This was it. He rapidly took the gun off "safe" and followed the crabbing target. It was going to be a rapidly changing deflection! Just as Len made the mental calculation to shoot at where the target would be when his shells got there, it seemed that the drogue got caught in a vortex, or some other capricious airflow, and brought the drogue to where he could have hit it with a thrown stone. Len squeezed out several short bursts—fearing that that which had made the target so plump might suddenly shift it to some more difficult angle. But no—it stood rock steady while he emptied his drum.

Sensing no more firing from the stern, Hamblyn waggled the wings of the *Battle*, and the trainees quickly moved to exchange places—although Len was reluctant to unfasten the safety harness without first checking if he could sense any further sudden movements of the airplane. Finally, they squeezed past one another, and Len watched LAC Richard take up his station and slap his ammunition drum smartly onto the machine gun. From his position crouched on the floor of the *Battle*, however, he could then see very little else. He was very happy about his shooting and was certain that the tally would show a good proportion of his shells had found their mark. That easily assuaged his consternation at nearly ending up as part of the scenery below.

While Len replayed the entire exercise in his head, he heard the warning horn sound—more clearly this time in the somewhat less wind-swept fuselage, and almost immediately Richie started firing. Soon, the acrid odour of cordite started to assault Len's nostrils, adding its pungency to the already pervasive glycol, gasoline, and hydraulic fluid. Abruptly, the shooting stopped and from the frantic movements above his head, Len knew that Richie was trying to sort out a jam in the machine gun. This was a constant problem, as the coloured dope they used to identify each trainee's shells often flaked off and made a mess of the internal mechanisms of the Vickers gun. Although he could not hear above the usual cacophony in the aircraft, Len knew that a string of invectives and epithets were being issued by his compatriot.

From the sudden lack of movement above, it was clear that Richie was again bringing his gun to bear on the target drogue, and he once again started to shoot. Several rhythmic bursts were issued, but between each, Richie's gesticulations grew more fervent. It was clear that he felt that he was not having a very good showing

Soon P/O Hamblyn was again waggling the wings, so Len knew that they would soon be landing. These exercises seldom lasted more than forty-five minutes, and that time was nearly up. Len felt several steep banks and turns and the unmistakable sound of the throttle being cut back as the pilot manoeuvred his kite to landing. Although his view was far more restricted than it was on takeoff, Len still felt the thrill of flight from his crouched position. Soon they had bounced onto the runway and were no doubt taxiing to their dispersal.

Both trainees boiled from the *Fairey Battle* as soon as it came to a rest. The ground crew sauntered to their tasks while P/O Hamblyn, now finished his cockpit duties, trudged toward the operations building. As with most of the RCAF pilots here, Hamblyn desperately wanted to get into operational flying against the enemy. He acted as if stooging around with these trainees was the furthest he could be from that, but he likely realized that his best chance was to keep doing his duty and hope that that would be considered when his requests for transfer were considered.

Richie was uncharacteristically silent while he and Len walked toward the huts to divest themselves of their now-empty ammunition drums. After that it would be back to the classroom for more calculations and aircraft identification exercises. Len was ecstatic about how the morning had finished. He could easily dismiss the "Incomplete" exercise from the earlier morning flight and his near-terminal plunge from the gun turret when he considered how many hits he was certain to have racked up with the fortuitous drogue positioning. But it was clear that his mate did not feel the same about his own performance. The lengthening lack of conversation grew uncomfortable.

"Thanks for the hand back there, Rich!" Len finally said. "I thought my number was up there for a second. How the heck did I forget to clip my safety harness?" It was a safe and sincere opening. Len truly was thankful and wanted Richie to know it.

Richie was forced to chuckle. "Damn straight, Len. Your luck nearly ran out there! It's just a good thing that I hate to fly alone." But then he turned sombre once again. "I just wish your goddamn luck would rub off on me now and again. I don't think I hit that flippin' target once today ... the drogue was all over the friggin' sky ... and all those cock-ups with the ammo? Shit! I will be lucky to not be washed out by Monday."

Len let Richie's self-directed diatribe trail off naturally. He felt it was prudent to not mention how well the exercise went for him, hoping to deflect the topic back to better things.

"Well, we won't be getting the scores back until late today at earliest, and I owe you at least a few rounds for your help today," Len offered. "It's Friday, and we'll surely go into town tonight." He hoped that the promised libations would distract Richie, but he knew from his own travails how it felt to be on tenterhooks awaiting the grim evaluations that dictated success or failure. They were in a shooting war, and there would be few allowances made—even for such a team-oriented and quick-thinking bloke like LAC Richard.

Richie only grunted in response. As they walked, Len heard a few more muttered oaths that were punctuated with rueful shakes of the head. The entire class of air gunner trainees were frequently told that they were one bad show from winding up sweeping floors or pushing paper at some backwater training camp in God-knows-where, Manitoba. It was probably meant as motivation by the instructors, but it seemed less inspirational than it was denigrating.

The two supplicants entered the hut to turn in the ammo drums that would be refilled for the next exercises. The corporal who was charged with receiving their kit was coincidentally the same man who would soon take charge of the target drogue and tally the holes it contained, each now identified with red and blue coloured flecks.

"LAC Richard," Len's mate intoned and then added almost in a whisper, "Red." The corporal recorded the name and colour of the .303 calibre shells that were used. Richie waited only long enough to see the information written and quickly turned on his heel. "See you at lunch, Len." And with that, he bolted from the building. The corporal barely raised an eyebrow at the display and turned to Len, who identified both himself and colour of ammunition used.

An inspiration then hit Len and he reached into his pocket to find the folded brown paper he carried for luck. "Moose Jaw money" is what they called it in Saskatchewan—a two-dollar banknote—so named because you could purportedly buy the services of a lady-of-the-evening on River Street in Moose Jaw for that price. Puritanical Prairie practice dictated that no self-respecting Saskatchewanian would have anything to do with such a cash denomination, but here in eastern Canada, it was commonly used. Len had been carrying the money every time he flew as a talisman, if for no other purpose. He surreptitiously slipped the cash under the canvas bag containing his ammo drum so that only a corner stuck out.

"Corporal? Can you look really hard to find red hits on our drogue today?" Len said quietly as he pushed the bag, drum, and bribe across the counter.

The corporal seemed confused at first—not by the payment, for it was almost a daily supplement to his pay from one trainee or another, but by other aspects of this transaction.

"Two bucks! Are you sure?" he answered in a hoarse whisper. The going rate was always a dollar or less, depending on the level of desperation. "And don't you mean, 'blue'?" he continued, pointing at the coloured remnants of paint littering the counter and the canvas of Len's ammo tote.

"No, I am certain that you will find as many reds as blue," Len said with a sly smile. As he left the somewhat bewildered but sated man, Len thought about luck. The best thing about it, he realized, was how easily it could be shared.

11

Mom put the sandwiches on the table, and the family was called for our usual post-church Sunday lunch. I was already seated in my spot in the place we called "the dining room," that was only a hallway leading from our front door. Every week this meal was a big deal, for we had all been fasting, as my father believed Roman Catholics should, for the entire morning before Mass. As usual, the entire family was present. We otherwise dined around the "kitchen table," but for this event, the table was moved and its leaf was installed.

The "feast" was usually modest, and today was no different—baloney sandwiches to be dipped into the healthy dollop of ketchup adorning each of our plates—washed down with plenty of milk. Dad, a dairy inspector by profession, ensured that we all knew the nutritional value of milk products. Although our other nutritional needs were likely not as well governed, we were always encouraged to drink milk for healthy "bone and teet." Although my father spoke with very little lingering French accent, the one phrase that betrayed his heritage and he seemed unable to master was "bones and teeth." Mom always teased him about that.

There was more teasing to come.

Conversation was often lively among the elders at the table. My older sisters and brothers were not shy in this comfortable company, and a wide variety of topics and banter was offered. I stayed quiet. After all, I was the second-youngest, and if I had not been specifically told what my social standing was in this family dynamic, I certainly felt it. In any case, I preferred to listen. I learned much more that way.

"Mom, what was that big 'thump' we heard in the middle of the night?" my eldest sister asked my parents. "It sounded like something hit the house!"

I had heard nothing that I remembered the previous night, but with eight people crammed into one small bungalow, one developed an ability to ignore sleep disturbances. I could easily conjure up hearing or not hearing it in my own recollection. Mom, however, clearly remembered and brought her closed first to her face to stifle her usual quiet chortle.

"That was your father falling out of bed!" Mom reported, still giggling in her demure way. "Were you dreaming about flying again, honey?"

Dad nodded in confirmation but said nothing to elaborate. The conversation quickly shifted to other fleeting topics, but my seven-year-old mind reeled with comic-book fantasies of flying superheroes and how I could easily identify with having such reverie. Perhaps Dad's reticence was because he was embarrassed to have such childish flights of fancy. Little did I suspect that the flying that he was undoubtedly imagining was done in the belly of a leviathan heavy bomber during the war, and not the carefree flight of a caped crusader. And with his silence, how could I even imagine that what he had experienced last night was more nightmare than dream?

"I wonder how far Paddy has got," Len said to no one in particular. He only just realized on speaking that it had been silent for several minutes. It was Stan that answered.

"He's probably sitting down to dinner by now at his mum 'n dad's place," Stan replied vacantly, while his gaze remained fixed on the same patch of floor that seemed to hold the interest of several of the crew. Paddy was the only original air gunner left on Robbie's crew, and he normally occupied the mid-upper turret. Len manned the rear turret of the Halifax. The two had become close—likely at first due to their similar responsibilities, but as their friendship grew, Len had found a man of similar temperament and values. Although the war had trained all of them to be parsimonious with friendships, it was always different within a crew.

Paddy was on leave. The entire crew was supposed to be on leave. Paddy was granted extra time to travel back to his home in Ireland so was gone in advance of the others. The rest were held back to be a reserve crew for this evening's operation. It was almost certain that they would not be needed. Indeed, it was looking less and less likely that the entire operation would go tonight. They were already past the briefed takeoff time, and the target for the night, Berlin, was a long trip at the best of times.

"Piss on it!" Pappy said as he jumped up. "I've had enough of this shit. I got things to do, people to see, and a pocket full of dough. I am outta here!" The crew's wiry Canadian navigator strode to the door. The remainder of the crew hardly flinched at this outburst. It was but his third one since they had been waiting. Only Bud, Paddy's replacement for tonight, seemed to take notice, following his earnest march toward the door.

At that very moment, Robbie, the crew's pilot and captain, re-entered the room with seemingly perfect timing to head off Pappy's escape. With him was another man whom Len did not recognize but who wore sergeant's stripes and pilot's wings.

"Going somewhere, Pappy?" Robbie asked in his usual off-hand manner.

"Just stretching my legs, Robbie," Pappy said, and he abruptly turned and headed back to a bench. The skipper watched with a smile that he shared with Len as their eyes met. Robbie would know his navigator was likely feeling the antsiest, for it was he who truly knew how to have a good time. Pappy, out of all of them, could best bend the rules and truly live the life of a free-spirited airman. Tonight was likely killing him. Robbie waited for him to settle again and then turned to the crew to speak. He seldom spoke above normal conversational volume, but the confident authority he exuded always elicited rapt attention.

"Boys, I have the latest gen. The lorry will be by in ten minutes to take us to dispersal. There have been more delays but the wingco wants us spring-loaded to go if the word comes through. I still don't think we're going, but we wouldn't want to be late joining the stream if we do, so let's get to it."

"I would also like to introduce you to Wilkie here, who is 'second dickey' tonight," Robbie continued. The squadron would normally send a sprog pilot on ops with an experienced crew shortly before or after a crew was posted to the station. The feeling was that seeing it all from an observer's position would ease a new pilot into a skipper's role. Len recalled that this wasn't a luxury afforded his first pilot when they arrived at RAF Lissett, but had become standard practice since. "Wilkie, Lofty is our engineer. Stan is our bomb aimer. Hale here is our W/Op." Warm handshakes and nods were exchanged quickly with each. "Len is our arse end, and Bud is filling in the other turret as our regular nimrod has left early on leave. You already ran into our nav, Pappy, the man who seems to always know where he is going."

There was a polite chuckle as the admonishing jibe set in and the final greeting handshakes were exchanged. There wasn't, however, a sound as they all moved to collect and don their kit. Len could almost sense their collective groan. You could tell that Robbie reckoned that they still would be scrubbed, for he was already dressed in what seemed to be his best uniform and had brought a grip with him from his barracks—fully expecting to go on leave from this room. He had told the group earlier that he had won a coin-toss with another crew as to which might be the reserve crew for tonight and who might be detailed for a training exercise over the Humber. He chose the former, knowing how unlikely it was that they would be needed. Everything that had happened since seemed to conspire against them, however. A trip out to the dispersal pan to wait it out under the wings of their bomber seemed to make it almost certain.

Len heard the low rumbling of the crew transfer lorry outside the building and knew that it was time to head out. In the near total darkness of the late January evening, the bright cheery smile of Len's favourite driver greeted each of them by name. Some of the WAAF personnel seemed almost afraid to speak with the men they ferried out to their aircraft—as if interaction might jinx the crew. Audrey was so much different. She had been at Lissett from the start and had driven countless crews, some only one way, but you always felt that she fully expected to drive you back to briefing upon your return. Len appreciated the confidence it instilled.

On the drive along the perimeter track to their bomber, Len tried to quell his unease over the pending operation. Maybe Robbie was right, and they would not be going. As many operations were cancelled as were mounted, and the delays so far this evening pointed to that eventuality. On the other hand, if they did end up going, the target for tonight was Berlin, and that could always be a shaky do. It would be his third trip to the "Big City," and he hadn't much enjoyed the previous two. Then again, there were not many of his twenty-three operations that had been cakewalks.

Audrey dropped them off at their usual dispersal where they found their ground crew tending *Jane,* the crew's Mark III Halifax bomber—barely broken in since arriving on station these past few weeks. The transfer wagon WAAF waved and shouted a warm "cheerio" to the crew as the lorry lurched away from the dispersal pan. Its dimmed-out headlight played briefly across the fuselage and the dimly painted aircraft identifier, "NP–J," painted across the side. The last thing the lorry's lights illuminated was the freshly painted image of *Jane,* the voluptuous and scantily clad heroine of the *Daily Mirror* newspaper cartoon pages. Len didn't know who, exactly, had painted her likeness, but this was a pleasing facsimile festooning the port fore side of the aircraft, just beneath the cockpit windows. It was at once risqué but comforting.

The crew gathered under the port wing to light up yet another cigarette. The cold, winter drizzle that had dampened the mood of the base earlier in the day had given way to a more pleasant south-westerly wind. It had failed to clear the overcast, but it made the late evening more pleasant to endure, especially as they were all cozily ensconced in their wool-lined flying kit. Here they waited for the inevitable word that their ops were cancelled, and they could finally start finding their way to their leave destinations off base.

Talk was about this and that, and Len didn't really join in. He looked at his watch and thought out loud more than spoke, "Too late to get anywhere tonight. There'll be no more trains anyway. They may as well have ops on."

"I wonder what the rail service is like in Sweden tonight," Bud said as an obvious attempt at black humour. It elicited a couple of wry chuckles from the crew, but Len never did much care for such japes. Why tempt the Fates when each crew had, at best, a one-in-twenty chance of not coming back from any operation?

There was a long silence after Bud's comment. After some time, there seemed to be some activity on the far side of Lissett aerodrome. A car seemed to be going from aircraft to aircraft, and soon the unmistakable sound of Bristol Hercules powerplants starting broke the relative quiet of the night air. It had taken a while to get used to the cacophony that erupted from these new, radial engines. They had a different pitch and timbre than the Merlin engines that powered the older Mark II Halifax, but their greater power seemed to make 158 Squadron's aircraft at least the equal of the vaunted Lancaster that the press always seemed to laud.

Robbie didn't turn his head as he watched what was happening and spoke matter-of-factly. "Well, lads, finish those smokes and have a pee, we may as well get started up." It was subtle, but Len could hear the disappointment in Robbie's voice. It was clear that the night's events had conspired against him, and as much as he didn't deserve to feel onus for this, Len knew him well enough to sense he would take this blame on top of all of his other responsibilities.

The time now flew in a flurry of activity as the air and ground crew paced through their pre-flight drills and checks. It seemed incongruous to Len how time could lengthen or shorten so capriciously, but it always flew when you were busy. Soon *Jane* was shaking with the engines running up to speed, through magneto drop checks and other list items. The ground crew stood flanking the aircraft. Abruptly the erk stationed at his port quarter position seemed to shout and pump his fist in the air, and only then did they start to move. Len had been curious about this behaviour that seemed to occur every time Robbie taxied out. He had eventually asked the groundcrew chief about it and heard that Robbie, with encouragement from all those left behind, would never start taxiing without paying special "homage" to the lady painted on the nose, just within his reach through the cockpit window. Robbie didn't seem to have many superstitions, but whatever rudeness or kindness that he showed to *Jane* seemed to work—they had always been safe.

Another check of his watch confirmed what Len had already known—it was after midnight as they taxied into position along the path to the downwind corner of the airfield. It had clearly taken them longer than usual to get squared away, for he could only make out one aircraft behind them. A long night was turning into a progressively longer one. Luckily, this was old hat to him—waiting was just another thing that the service had taught him. He listened to the usual chatter on the intercom but felt no need to participate beyond what was *de rigueur*. Experience had taught him that, too.

It was finally their turn to turn upwind, and he more felt than heard the familiar rumble of four engines being run up to near impossible speed, and then the sudden lurch as the brakes were released. The different power plants in this fresh bomber certainly seemed to get them up to speed much more quickly, but the roll to takeoff still seemed interminable. Len felt the tail wheel beneath him lift from the concrete as *Jane* reached critical velocity, and soon the rhythmic thuds of concrete joints passing under wheels disappeared as the kite lifted from the earth. No matter how many times he had experienced it, Len never failed to be exhilarated by this leap from the ground, for now he was counted separately from the rest of humanity—those who were aloft versus those still earthbound.

The climb out gave time to think. Once the imminent hazard of getting tons of metal and high explosives airborne was completed, there was little for the gunners to do until over enemy territory. Certainly they would check their guns and do all they could to mentally prepare for the night ahead, but the truth was that they could best serve their crewmates by simply keeping silent vigil. Len, during his time flying as a "spare" on other crews, had sometimes been tasked to drop and follow wind drift markers to aid navigation. On this crew, however, Pappy seemed so supremely confident in his navigation skills and equipment that it had never been needed. As much as their navigator was euphemistically described as "a character" on the ground— "shit disturber" was likely more apt—he was a more than competent component of the crew. Indeed, every member of this crew were men of such loyalty, dedication, and duty that Len could not think of a better group. Or was this feeling only the natural outgrowth of having put your life in their hands and theirs in yours?

The long trek over the North Sea gave plenty of time to mull such thoughts. Len was certain that they were not going to be flying tonight and so scarcely paid attention during briefing, but he still recalled the bright red tape of the planned route laid nearly straight east from Lissett across Denmark and then directly southeast to Berlin. Their return trip was to be nearly reciprocal. It was promised to be largely free of fighters save for those based en route, and maybe those that they were certain to encounter over the German capital. Len knew well enough that Intelligence often made a cock-up of what was to be expected and so mixed his deep thoughts with a healthy portion of sky-scanning vigilance.

The outbound trip proved to be largely uneventful. Len's pulse quickened somewhat as he saw some distant combats, but they all seemed rather short and thankfully without the large explosion that would terminally end a bomber crew's tour. He also noted in his peripheral vision the searchlights paired with the flak batteries near Sylt—their probing shafts of light occasionally piercing the broken cloud. He said a silent prayer of thanks that this menace was comfortably to the south of their track.

Now that they were over enemy-occupied territory, the traffic on the intercom took on a far more serious tone. As was his wont, Len seldom chimed in unless asked, but he was somewhat amused that it seemed even more businesslike than usual while they had on board the sprog pilot as "second dickie." Even Pappy gave clipped, efficient information. Everyone was always on their best behaviour when there was company in the house! They would do their best to return Wilkie to his regular crew after showing him the best example of a bomber operating at peak efficiency.

Len continued his scan of the sky. Both he and Bud, in the mid-upper turret, reported to their skipper when they saw something of note. Obviously, there were fighters lurking, but you needn't worry too much about ones out of range of the guns in their turrets unless they stalked or positioned to attack. The German cannon and machine guns had a far greater range, so experience taught that you never gave away your position by firing at night fighters outside the reach of your .303 Brownings. Bud, on only his third sortie, seemed a bit antsier and called out even the most distant contacts. Len would have felt more secure with his friend and far more experienced gunner, Paddy, in the top turret, but the replacement was starting in a good place. It was far better to be too cautious than not.

The bursts of flak were now getting far more frequent as they neared the target. The acrid waft of the cordite in the spent shells tickled Len's nose. The capricious nature of antiaircraft artillery almost seemed more malevolent than the fighters that were dedicated to seeking out and destroying. The bursts that at first seemed random were now ever increasing in their accuracy. On their run-up to the centre of Berlin, their aiming point, Robbie, in the pilot's seat, could no longer dodge and weave and skip and jump to off put the predicted flak. He was now simply following the instructions of Stan at the bomb aimer's station. Len could hear Stan's monotonous intonations clearly on the 'com.

"Steady, Skipper ... steady ... steady ..." Len listened raptly. He once worried when their run-up was so free of corrections by the pilot, for it might allow the flak batteries' calculations to hone in the aircraft much more precisely. But there were so many variables with flak, it didn't pay to dwell on it. *Jane* seemed to almost sigh as its load of high explosives and incendiaries were loosed down on the target that had seemed to be sending so much upwards.

"Bombs gone!" There was a hint of triumph in Stan's even delivery of the report.

In an instant the world seemed to disappear in a blinding flash of light and searing pain as Len was knocked senseless for several moments. He could not make out what had happened, for everything seemed to be different—replaced with an ethereal haze, fierce buffeting, and deafening noise. Although his vision was gone, he saw clearly the faces of his mother and father in his mind's eye. Was this what it was like to die?

The explosion had robbed him of his vision and hearing. Several places on his body felt as if they had been pierced with a hot poker. Slowly, order seemed to come back as Len put the evidence together. The white noise cacophony subsided, and his sight started to return as he furiously blinked to clear it. What he saw, heard, and felt did nothing to slacken the pace of his heart, already threatening to leap from his chest.

The slipstream of the Halifax seemed to assault him from all sides, and he realized that almost all the Perspex that had formed the transparent plastic cocoon of his turret had disappeared. Len, like most rear turret air gunners, had worked with the ground crew to remove the centre panel to afford better visibility. Now all of it was gone. Through the shattered remnants of the plastic and metal frame, Len could just make out what was left of his Browning guns—one was canted at an unnatural and useless angle while another was shorn off at mid length. It was clear that he could no longer offer any resistance to any enemy fighter attack from astern.

They had been hit by an exploding flak shell. That much was clear. Len released his death grip on the turret controls. He had no idea how much further damage had been done to his trusty Bolton-Paul turret and didn't dare manipulate it for fear it might just pack up and fall off the aircraft with him sealed inside. He flexed his hands and his lower legs and was treated to the exquisite pain that must accompany being violated by sharp shards of hot metal. The pain in his left palm was especially bad, and he felt a warm, sticky wetness beginning to spread in his heavy, lined gloves.

As his hearing returned, he was somewhat relieved to recognise the dull drone of *Jane's* engines. The aircraft still seemed to be flying, thank God, but the engines sounded different. Perhaps this was just the way they sounded when their roar was not deadened by an intact turret. When Len was certain that his hearing had returned, he tried the intercom.

"Rear gunner to Skipper," he croaked out with forced calm. "Rear gunner to captain." Silence answered. "Rear gunner to crew." Again, there was no response.

Len tried to make out the extent of damage in the dim light outside his turret. Down below, the ground was illuminated by hundreds of flashes from falling ordnance and the unmistakable glow of fires burning on the ground beneath the clouds. He could just make out some of the bomber's control surfaces on the tail, but after observing them for a few moments, they did not seem to be moving. Finding the dull separation that he knew marked the horizon outside the aircraft, he could tell that they seemed to be flying tail-heavy, as if in trying to climb.

The air gunner in the rear turret normally had the most solitary job on a heavy bomber, but at this moment, Len had never felt more alone. He had no idea if his crewmates were injured, dead, or had all abandoned the airplane. All he knew was that it was still flying. He chose to take that as a positive sign as he sat in what was left of his station at the aft end of the bomber. He tried the intercom several more times with still no response. The turret seemed to creak and groan as it was jostled by the buffeting air around it. Len suddenly felt as unsafe, as he was alone. He whipped off his oxygen mask and scrambled into the dubious safety of *Jane's* fuselage. By sheer muscle memory, he grabbed his parachute from its stowage just outside of his turret, knelt, and clipped it to the harness he wore. In the haziness that was clouding his mind, he briefly checked if it was undamaged from the explosion. It seemed intact. Without oxygen, however, he just felt the need to sleep. Curled into a ball against the cold, he let the comfort of hypoxic unconsciousness overtake him.

Waves seemed to wash over him as consciousness returned. In the dim light he could make out the concerned face of Lofty, the flight engineer, who seemed to be pressing an oxygen mask close to Len's face. Len felt his eyes flutter several times, and things became more focussed. They were in *Jane's* rest area. How he had gotten here was anyone's guess, but he knew for certain he hadn't done it alone.

"Are you with us again, mate?" Lofty shouted over the still droning engines. Len could only nod as Lofty took the oxygen mask away and took several deep breaths from it himself. He then offered it to Len, who once again availed himself of the replenishing gas. It was clear that they were still at altitude and needed to share the engineer's mask. Len's oxygen apparatus was left plugged into the rear turret supply, and it was quite likely damaged by the explosion. This would help explain his rash actions in the wake of the explosion. It was also clear that no-one was going to chance going back to retrieve it in any case.

When Lofty was once again free of the mask, he leaned in and shouted, "Wilkie patched y'up best he could, and it don't look too bad, but you gave us a fright." Len only noticed now that his left glove had been removed and a dressing tied to his palm. He assumed that the dull pain in his legs had received similar ministrations. "The intercom r'out and y'know the rear turret is 'U/S' and we have some damage to the tail, but Wilkie's helping the skipper wrestle d'kite. Jammy thing we had a second dickie t'night, wot? Pappy has given a course back t'base and Bud is watchin' fer fighters. We might just come outta dis scrape ok." He slapped Len on the shoulder to punctuate the assessment.

Lofty once again took the mask and gulped heavily from it. Len took the opportunity to find his glove and slipped his bandaged hand back into its cold stiffness. The rest area was heated in the Halifax, which is to say that some waste heat from the engines was piped to the location. It was still draughty and cold, but it was miles ahead of what he had in his turret—even when it wasn't shot through with holes!

At altitude it didn't take long to feel the effects of the lack of oxygen. All aircrew were well versed in recognizing the signs of hypoxia—certainly in each other, because one's own impaired judgement as to its onset was one of the first symptoms. Len remembered well the annotation in his logbook that denoted the result of his own high-altitude training. It seemed he succumbed to the effects more severely than many of his compatriots. It never held him back, because he was always careful with his oxygen supply. Tonight, however, was going to be a continuing challenge.

"Take a good slug, Len," Lofty shouted to his injured compatriot. "I oughta go check the gauges and tanks, so you'll be on y'r own for wee bit."

Len held the mask to his face for some time and breathed deeply. He had settled down quite a bit since leaving his turret, although he couldn't escape a twinge of guilt at leaving his post—and by extension his crewmates—undefended. This was quickly extinguished as he realized that he had no choice—the turret was unserviceable. Flexing his left hand, he realized that the turret's gunner was also in a similar state.

Lofty simply watched Len look back, still breathing from the mask. In the several minutes that passed, Lofty's countenance morphed from quiet concern to impish grin. Len had seen this look on the diminutive engineer's face before, but only after several rounds of bitter at the Brunswick. While many other people deprived of sufficient oxygen would turn belligerent, Len reckoned that Lofty was a "happy hypoxic."

Len saw Lofty disconnect the mask from the rest area connection and took it with him as he nimbly scrambled over spar and past equipment back to his station behind Robbie. If there was a perfect physical build for a flight engineer, Lofty certainly had it. Len could only watch the flurry of activity forward. In the dimness of the bomber's interior, he could just make out Robbie's head and shoulders. Beside him, it must be Wilkie in close contact, or even leaning over the skipper. Lofty was moving from side to side behind them and apparently talking with both. Aft of the rest area, Len could make out the lower half of Bud in the mid-upper turret, spinning his seat from side to side and even facing it forward as he maintained his vigilance. He was the only real defence against enemy aircraft attack, but the truth be known, if they were attacked from underneath or astern, he may as well be in the rest area with Len.

Len grew less and less concerned with anything that was happening around him. Lofty had been gone for a few minutes, and he was undoubtedly feeling the effects of the thin air once again. But there was no other way. The engineer must tend to the petrol usage. Tanks must be emptied evenly, or the aircraft was difficult to handle, and this was likely made more critical by the damage they had sustained. Lofty mentioned nothing about damage to fuel tanks, so Len imagined they would have enough to make it back to England.

When Lofty returned they again took turns with the oxygen mask. It wasn't quite the same as a constant supply, but it at least kept them conscious. An added benefit was that they both seemed to be taking almost drunken pleasure in their predicament. Perhaps, thought Len, that that might be a detriment. But that only occurred during the times he was breathing with aid of the mask—while Lofty grew progressively sillier without it.

The engineer left Len at the rest position several more times as he continued to monitor the progress and health of their sick aircraft. Len felt like they must be losing height, because his hypoxic symptoms seemed to be diminishing. Either that or he was becoming acclimated. They had been flying a long time, and a check of his watch confirmed this. Although the engines sounded different, Len assumed it was only because he was hearing it from this unfamiliar vantage—they certainly seemed to be running smoothly.

Lofty made his way back again.

"You oughta be okay now," he yelled. "Skipper's got us down to eleven. I gotta keep a close eye on things, so you'r be okay here?" he finished, half statement/half question.

"Yeah, sure," Len replied with a nod and unconsciously looked down at his aching hand. "How much longer you figure it'll be?"

"It's gonna be another hour," Lofty replied without further elaboration, and he quickly turned to move up front again.

Another hour! Len thought as he again checked his watch. It was already 0630, and they had left the target three hours ago. They must be over the North Sea by now. The mere thought of that inky cold blackness gave him a shudder. Almost anything would be preferable to ditching in the ocean in January, even if their dinghy was undamaged by the explosion. Waiting another hour didn't seem so bad after all.

Suddenly there was a flurry of activity at the pilot's station as Robbie seemed to struggle with the controls, and Len felt the kite shift under him. The reasons for this evasion became pointedly clear an instant later as the unmistakable sound of shells thudded through the aircraft. Len saw no frantic movement of the top turret or return fire response, so it seemed that the damage was being inflicted from below, where Bud's gun could not depress to return fire. Was it friendly fire from a light flak battery on the English coast? Couldn't they respond with the "colours of the day" to indicate that they were an RAF plane? They couldn't still be over enemy territory, could they?

With some trepidation, Len got up and moved back past Bud's turret to the rear of the aircraft. In the darkness he could make out a few new holes, some exactly where his parachute had been stowed. He said a quick prayer that his training had drilled into him that he should never leave the tail without it. The rear hatch also looked like it had taken damage, and it was no longer an option for leaving the kite, but there appeared to be no critical components hit. Just being in the rear compartment brought back the events of what had occurred over the target, so he quickly moved forward once again. At the rest area he met up with Stan, who likely had been sent back to assess any further damage. Stan's primary duty as the air bomber likely made his contributions up front largely redundant, and with everyone else busy, he was the logical choice.

"Nuthin' serious, Stan," Len leaned to intone in his ear. "But we're startin' t'look like a target drogue back there and the rear hatch is duff. Wizard thing they can't shoot straight! Was it Home Guard shooting at us?"

Stan eyes just widened as he shook his head fractionally and he leaned in to shout back at Len, who canted his head to hear. "That was Jerry light flak. We're still o'er Germany." And he turned to return forward to make his report.

Len's heart sank. Were they flying in circles? How could they still be over Germany? What was going on? He slumped onto the cold-hardened cushions covering the rest area benches and checked his watch once again. It was nearly 0700. They had been airborne for nearly six and a half hours. Even on a long flight with Berlin as target, they would not have more fuel for more than eight hours of flying. And soon dawn would make them easy prey for more light flak, or even fighters.

It seemed a long time before Stan returned.

"Skipper's made it to Holland an' e's given the word. We've only got juice to get arfway cross the drink n' so we're bailin' out." Stan paused and then shrugged. There was really nothing more to say about it. "You go get Bud outta there and start moving up." And with that he started his own movement up toward the forward hatch.

Len felt like he should sit and contemplate the enormity of what Stan had just said, but there wasn't time for that. Now his responsibility to his crewmates kicked in and he moved to the mid-upper turret where Bud had been continuing his lonely vigil. Len moved beside the still turning turret and grabbed the man's knee as it swung past. He could feel Bud startle slightly at the touch—not surprisingly after so many solitary hours on duty. Bud leaned down and cocked his head to hear.

"Time to go, Bud. Skipper's given the word. Bailing out over Holland," Len said with as much authority and calm as he could muster. Bud, for his part, seemed much less surprised at the news than Len had been. Obviously his 360° vantage on the top side of the aircraft had told him more about their current situation than had Len's, ensconced in the belly of the Halifax.

The order had been given, but there didn't appear to be a rush to the exit, so Len waited for Bud to extricate himself from the turret and retrieve his own parachute. It too seemed to be undamaged. The two then made their way forward to the escape hatch that was located under the navigator's table. They squeezed past Lofty, still on duty at his station behind the pilot's seat, still occupied by their stalwart pilot. Robbie seemed hunched into some facsimile of a pretzel while pushing the control column forward. It was clear at once that *Jane* had been fighting him all these many hours. She was more damaged than Len imagined. Len clasped Robbie on the thigh as he manoeuvred past and then turned to give him a "thumbs-up." His captain only gave him a curt nod and turned his attention back to grappling with the recalcitrant controls. Outwardly, he appeared calm and in control as always, but Len could sense that the strain of keeping them airborne this long was beginning to show.

In the front compartment, Bud and Len found a tremendous wind blast emanating from the detached emergency hatch. Stan and Hale had apparently already exited the aircraft. Wilkie was on the floor eyeing the open hatch. Pappy stood as if he was a trolley conductor. He held out his hand.

"Tickets, please!" Pappy, grinning, shouted over the cacophony that filled the draughty compartment. "If you don't have a ticket, I'll have to put you off the bus," he warned as he jerked a thumb toward the hatch, and then he cackled as only Pappy could.

It wasn't that the humour was unappreciated, but Len was transfixed by what was going on in front of him and what he must now do. He watched as Wilkie leapt, feet first, through the hatch. Strangely, his drop seemed to stop with only his head and shoulders bobbing frantically in the slipstream, blocking the hatch. Some protrusion had caught the collar of his Mae West and he was hung up. Bud moved quickly forward and unceremoniously pushed Wilkie out of the hatch with the sole of his flying boot and then turned to Pappy and Len watching and gave a slight shrug, although no explanation was necessary. The man had been blocking their only exit.

Bud then crouched and jumped, leaving only Lofty and Robbie in the cockpit and Pappy and Len in the forward fuselage. Pappy gestured to Len that he should go first, and Len could only nod in response. He was shaking with fear as he approached the dim rectangle that seemed to be growing impossibly small as he approached. Despite witnessing two others exit in front of him, Len suddenly worried that he might not fit through it. His mind inexplicably flitted back to something told him in training—that if your head fit through an opening, the rest of your body would too. This one shred of gen seemed to be enough to give impetus, for he quickly knelt to the hatch and dove head first into the predawn murk below.

Len tumbled once and then twice as the fierce wind blast changed from lateral to upwards as he lost forward velocity and gained some with his descent. He knew that *Jane* had been losing altitude steadily, so he must not delay in deploying his parachute. He gave the chute release a firm yank and there was a jarring jolt of deceleration as the canopy filled—it felt as if his arms and legs would detach from his body as the harness dug into his shoulders and crotch. He could hear the Halifax's engines droning on into the distance. Craning his neck, he tried to discern the aircraft or his crewmate's parachutes but could make nothing out. He said a prayer for his three friends left on the plane that they too had exited shortly after.

Despite his earlier trepidation, Len now found the parachute descent strangely tranquil. He could tell it was very windy, but after the bone-rattling seven-hour flight shot through with genuine terror and injury, now ending with his rollicking plunge from the stricken kite, this was quite peaceful, indeed. Len surveyed the ground below and it seemed from this perspective, and illuminated by the pre-dawn sky glow, to be very much like the farm fields of southern Saskatchewan. It was interspersed with drainage ditches, but it was pleasingly flat and devoid of trees.

As the ground rushed up at Len, he tried desperately to recall what minimal training he had had in this. It now seemed all too obvious that aircrew, and especially air gunners, would never be expected to make it this close to successfully surviving having their aircraft shot down. "Assume a sitting position when landing" was all that seemed to stick in his mind. That was easier said in a classroom than accomplished out here with a chunk of enemy-occupied territory and an entirely uncertain future rushing up to meet you!

Somehow Len managed to brace himself sufficiently against the landing as he alighted near a road in a farmer's plowed, fallow field. It was soft, if somewhat muddy. He managed to spill his parachute and get it off in good order, and he then recalled what else he had been told if ever he should find himself in this situation—remain calm, take time to light a cigarette, and plan your next actions. He reached into his flying suit and found in his tunic where he stashed his package of Sweet Caps. By the time he took one out and put it between his lips, it seemed that all the strain, fear, terror, and pain of the last eight hours came quickly to a head. He began to shake uncontrollably. It started in his thighs and spread to his chest, neck, and arms so that when he attempted to light his cigarette, the match kept going out from the shaking.

Finally getting the smoke lit, he took a deep draw, but it did not have the same calming effect that so many previous post-landing cigarettes had. He watched in fascination, as he could see some distance in this flat land, a vehicle approaching. Obviously if he could see them, his parachute descent must have been easily discernible. As it approached, Len could see that it was of a completely unfamiliar, foreign design but patently military in appearance and colour. It stopped on the nearby road, and two men exited. The driver stood by his open door while the passenger walked slowly toward Len. As he neared, Len could make out the uniform. The rifle carried casually at the soldier's hip was pointed at his chest.

Len put the cigarette in his mouth and slowly raised his hands above his head. The soldier spoke through a thick German accent the only words of English that he had been taught.

"For you, the war is over."

12

"Son, could you get me a drink of water?"

My father sat in the easy chair under the pole lamp in our living room, reading the evening newspaper. I had been reading a book in another corner of the room and had noticed that he had only recently sat down. Dad was a firm but fair disciplinarian, so he could always reasonably expect his edicts to be carried out. It scarcely mattered. At my tender age of six, I was still in hero-worshipping awe of the man and would have likely moved the house had he asked me.

I arose but said nothing. I knew that no response was necessary once he saw me act. It was a scant few steps in our small home to the kitchen and the drinking water faucet. The cupboard over the counter where all our dishware was stored was always a challenge for me given my small stature. It usually entailed pushing one of our chrome set chairs to the sink and using its height advantage to obtain even a drinking glass. I had seen my older brother, for years, muscle up onto the counter like a gymnast and obtain a glass that way, but my similar efforts were always thwarted by my scrawny arms—much to his teasing glee.

I ascended the chair and turned on the water to let it run, for Dad always liked his water cold. Opening the cupboard to get a tumbler yielded a surprise: a completely incongruous and sweet surprise! There, just adjacent to the door catch, was a small roll of sugar candies, pristine in their cellophane wrap. I surveyed the kitchen, but I was the only one there. After a second glance over each shoulder, I slipped the sweet treasure trove surreptitiously into my pants pocket. I quickly filled a glass, replaced the chair, and delivered the water to my father, of course saying nothing.

I made good my escape into our shared, but deserted, boys' bedroom, where I savoured each and every piece of candy. Sweets were not common in our house, and with five siblings, sharing usually meant for a meagre portion. My abject guilt was easily assuaged by the solitary enjoyment of this delectable treat. Too soon it was gone and with studied calm, I returned to the book I had left in the room where my father sat, still reading the newspaper.

"Son?" I jumped at the sound of his voice, feeling that the jig was now up. "Could you put my glass in the sink?"

My casual response belied my quickened pulse, but now I sensed that I had successfully gotten away with my ill-gotten booty. I retrieved the tumbler to take to the kitchen. Although I likely could have reached to put the glass in the sink, once again I dragged the chair over to the counter. Completing my job, I could not resist opening the cupboard one more time—either to relive the feeling of finding my treasure or perhaps to see if I had missed anything. To my mounting excitement, there was another roll of candy! In precisely the same place! How could I have missed that! Again, I did a quick check in both directions but was given a start when I looked toward the living room. There was my father, newspaper folded on his lap, craning to peek at me through the doorway leading to the kitchen. He quickly sat back, but not before I saw his eyes twinkling and a wide grin on his face. I felt far less compunction as I secreted the second roll of candies in my pocket.

The vehicle slithered and slid precariously along the muddy roads as the driver ignored all harbingers of their impending demise. Len's mind reeled with how he had experienced so many new things in just the past few hours. As if being wounded by enemy shrapnel and having to parachute out of a crippled Halifax bomber wasn't enough! Now it seemed that after surviving all that, he would die rather prosaically in a sodden ditch in occupied Holland because of the maniacal ministrations of his German captors. All he had ever prayed for was a good death. This would not qualify.

The rifle of the man in the back seat wasn't exactly pointed at his ribs, but there didn't seem to be much guarantee that if they fishtailed again, its discharge wouldn't be lethal. Len looked at the guard in the early light of this late January morning. The German, with a dark uniform that Len found as strange as the rest of the surroundings, smiled wanly at him, and shouted something to the driver in front. It was clearly not a request to be more careful, for the man in control of this canvas topped convertible seemed to gun the engine harder. Len did not return the smile, for it seemed less friendly than it was smug and self-satisfied.

Although the breakneck course they were forging seemed to rivet his attention, Len could not help but wonder what had become of his crewmates. He had seen too many Hollywood films of parachute drops where soldiers landed within earshot of one another. Bailing out of a stricken heavy bomber in the scarcely discernible predawn light was clearly another matter. He saw no evidence of his companions on the way down. Where they had landed or if their parachutes had functioned properly was as much a mystery as the fate of the mighty but mortally wounded aircraft that he had abandoned.

The car careened around another sharp turn. The driver then sped down another long straightaway. These roads of Holland were more like the roads of his home in rural Saskatchewan than the winding or gently curving motorways of England. There were strangely spaced trees along the path and much lower hedgerows than what he had become familiar with in East Yorkshire. The flatness was familiar, but the flora was foreign. He stared out at yet another field rushing past him and thought of home and how the news of his disappearance would be received by his family. He had lived—when for months he was certain that he would die. Now he knew that he must somehow get word to them that he was okay.

From the gathering gloomy light of this overcast morning and despite the frequent changes of direction, Len could tell that they were heading generally southwest. The brightest sky was behind them. The vehicle's speed bled off as the rural vista turned to a thickening density of buildings. It seemed to be a town of moderate size. Len hoped that this was their destination, for another leg at the mercy of this dubiously-skilled chauffeur might be his last.

They passed slowly through the midst of several official-looking buildings, many of which were festooned with bright, red German pennants and other trappings of the hated Nazi regime. If this was meant to intimidate, it was certainly doing its job, for Len felt his guts clench. The enormity of the situation now filled him with dread. He was a captive and *persona non grata*. The only saving grace was that Robbie had managed to pilot the airplane to a setting where the enemy was but an occupation force and the locals might be sympathetic. It would have been far worse to have landed in the midst of fanatical German civilians that he had been party to bombing. He tried to take a calming deep breath, but it rasped in his throat. The guard beside him shook his head in a clear warning for Len to stay silent.

When they had lurched to a stop, the driver exited, and after a few guttural shouts to other uniformed men in the compound, jerked open the door beside Len.

"Raus!" the man shouted with undue authority. Len rose unsteadily while his backseat guard exited behind him. The driver led them into the building, where his captors gave a somewhat lengthy report to the apparent amusement of the officer seemingly in charge. The room had several desks and tables, about half of which were occupied by what appeared to be administrative soldiers. At least they appeared to be of that ilk, for the only intimidating presence in the room were the man in charge and two rather stoic guards standing at a vague approximation of "stand easy" with a rifle. Len's initial captors waited until their names were recorded before they were dismissed. Perhaps some bounty or honour was due them for their intrepid duty. Len felt they might all deserve a gong for only surviving the car ride!

The officer casually moved toward Len.

"How many on your aircraft?" The officer had a slight accent but spoke very passable English.

The query initially caught Len off guard. He had expected that matters of identity would be taken care of first, so after a pause to compose his best approximation of calm delivery, he spoke directly to the far wall, giving only his full name, rank, and service number. They had been drilled incessantly throughout training and with numerous reminders while on station at RAF Lissett that that was all they were required to provide the enemy.

The officer sighed. "We want to know so that if any of your companions were injured or in need of assistance, we might be able to help them." To Len's fatigue-addled mind, this sounded somewhat reasonable and compassionate. Luckily, his rote training forestalled this crude attempt to garner intelligence. He simply stared forward and repeated the scant information required.

The officer was staring at him for several seconds and then, with some resignation, gestured to one of the men at a desk who sat ready to copy the information. Len dutifully repeated his identification slowly and carefully, this time spelling his name.

"Fold your pockets to the outside," the officer ordered. He seemed to have lost some of the civility that he had shown earlier. It took a moment for the strange structure of the command to sink in. Len saw the guards tense slightly as he reached toward his tunic, as if the delay was perceived as either reluctance or perhaps subterfuge. He paused in an exaggerated sense to prove that there was no threat and then slowly continued. Len, unlike some of his compatriots, generally followed standard orders that they fly on operations with nothing in their pockets. The only illicit goods he had was his package of Canadian cigarettes, Sweet Caps, some matches, and the rosary that he always carried with him. Also dug from his pocket was the RAF-issued escape kit—a cellophane pouch cleverly packed with maps, foreign currency, provisions, and several other doodads. He would have rather gotten rid of this before this time, but his quick capture had precluded that. He felt some guilt as the officer snatched it up and started pawing through its contents.

Almost absently, the officer spoke in German, and one of the two guards stepped forward and gestured to Len with his gun that he should move toward the door. Len turned to the officer, still rapt with the intricacies of the escape kit, screwed up his courage and asked, "May I have my rosary?"

"*Nein,*" came the stern, even reply. The man did not even look up.

The portal that Len now moved toward was opened by the remaining guard. The parade of three, with Len sandwiched between, now walked down a short corridor until the leading soldier stopped and unlocked a heavy door, opened it, and stepped to one side. Len understood what was required and stepped in. He saw that it was a moderately large, empty cell. He heard the door lock behind him. He stood for just a few seconds and looked around, but the spartan fixtures demanded no appraisal. He walked to the far wall and sat on the floor.

As he sat, he realized how much he had been running on adrenaline. He winced as he shifted his legs into a more comfortable position. He had not really checked the extent of the wounds he had received when the flak knocked out his turret. He was not going to reveal to his captors that he had suffered any ill effect—he would not give them the satisfaction—although they had taken a cursory look under the dressing on his palm. Now alone, he could assess the damage in some privacy. The punctures on his legs were not large and seemed to have stopped bleeding. He cinched the dressing ties tight again, just in case. The one on his left palm, however, still hurt like hell and threatened to at least ooze blood whenever he moved his hand. Worse still, there was no sign of an exit wound, so the sharp metal must still be imbedded. The only thing he knew for sure was that he wasn't going to count on the Germans for help. He tried to elevate his injured hand on his chest, leaned back, and closed his eyes.

He must have dozed, for he awoke to the sound of shouts and commotion in the hall outside the cell. The door rattled, and Len did his best to jump to his feet, although the pain that shot through his lower legs reminded him that that was likely not a good idea. Through the open doorway moved Wilkie, the second pilot from their Berlin raid. Although they had first met scant hours ago, Len still couldn't help feeling relief that this face was at least vaguely familiar. He was also overjoyed to learn that he was not the sole survivor. Len quickly composed himself, determined to not convey any untoward information with a friendly greeting or even recognition. The door slammed shut again and was locked. In short order, a panel covering an opening in the door slid open and an eye and then an ear alternately appeared.

Wilkie appeared quite a sight. Every limping step seemed to be accompanied by a wince. His clothing was muddied and wet. He managed to make his way to one of the low, wide benches that sat along the outside walls of the cell. Len only realized at this moment that these were likely designed to be beds. The new arrival shuffled to the one farthest from the door and plopped down upon it. Len chose to again sit on the floor beside him. They sat in silence until their watcher seemed to give up and the panel slid closed once again.

"Good to see ya, mate," Wilkie said, *sotto voce*. "How's the wing and undercarriage?" He gestured to Len's wounded limbs.

"Thanks for patching me up," Len replied in a similar whisper out the side of his mouth. The stab of pain as he began to flex his injured hand cut off the demonstration that he was all right. "I don't think there's any serious damage done. Have you seen anyone else?"

"Nary a soul. I went out after the W/Op and the air bomber but got hung up. They would have landed well behind me. Was it you that shoved me out?"

"Nah, that was Slim. Your Mae West was caught. I hope that you didn't need it." Len gestured to the still nearly dripping-wet pants legs.

"The ruddy ditch I landed in wasn't that deep, but I was thankful for the shove. I was fairly well thrashed against the belly of the kite. I'll have bruises from chin to toes." Wilkie vaguely stretched his arms and grimaced in either pain or remembrance of hanging outside the still-flying bomber.

"Hell of a first trip for ya, eh?"

"Aye. On the run-up, I saw a flak burst three miles ahead, right on line, and then one about half that distance on the same line, so I knew the next one was gonna be close. But I kept hearing 'Steady ... Steady ...'" Wilkie trailed off, because he knew nothing more need be said—especially since it was Len who bore the brunt of the last shell.

After an uncomfortable pause, the two continued their whispered banter. The talked about nothing, really, except to get to know each other. Occasionally, the sliding hatch in the cell door would open and an eye or ear would admonish them back into mute reticence. The conversation would eventually continue once the observer retreated. Their dialogue, however, could be that of two strangers, for that is essentially what they were.

This time there was no warning when the door was unlocked and flung open. To appear nonchalant, but likely in deference to their weariness, the current denizens of the holding cell did not rise. After yet another guttural shout from someone unseen, the two new captives entered rather spritely. In the otherwise gloomy cell, their eyes came afire with recognition of the two already held. Len stared at them blankly, hoping to convey that silence was the prudent modus at present. Still, Len was over the moon to see the hearty faces of Stan and Hale.

Although the door slammed shut again after the two new captives, the surveillance panel was still open. The crew's air bomber and wireless operator stood apart from Len and Wilkie, in whispered conversation, only occasionally stealing glances over to the others. They both looked none the worse for wear. Indeed, Stan looked as if he had just come off parade. Len had spent enough time with Hale to know that his current proud bearing was only in defiance of his captors. His tousled blond hair framed a face of abject weariness and strain.

"Shall we introduce ourselves to these sods?" Hale said to his companion, in an almost comically loud voice. He and Stan sauntered over to where Len was seated. Although the acting was bad, Len sensed that the ruse had worked, or the guards had given up trying to gain any gen from this lot, for the door's panel slid shut once more.

As soon as they sensed they were not being watched, Len joined all three in breaking into wide grins. With muted expressions of "Attaboy!" and "Wizard!" exchanged between the reunited crew, it was clear that each was very relieved to see that others had made it out. The quartet exchanged a quick recount of how they had been captured. It seemed that none of them had much of a chance to evade—not with their shot-up Halifax's engines droning rather low over the occupied Dutch towns. Len's capture, though, seemed the quickest, with the other three at least encountering some rather skittish civilians who seemed sympathetic, but nonetheless wary, about helping downed Allied airmen.

"I wonder how the others made out," Hale wondered aloud.

"It was only Pappy, Lofty, and the skipper left when I went out," Len offered. "Slim went out just before I did, and he had just *helped* Wilkie out." Len, at this, winked at Wilkie, not mentioning what was essentially a stomp to the second pilot's head after he had become ensnared in the escape hatch on his bail out.

"Robbie sure was fighting the old kite," Stan said, "but he kept it steady for us."

There were murmurs of assent, but the conversation seemed to stall as they silently considered the fate of the pilot, engineer, and navigator that they knew to have still been on the bomber when they left. Left unspoken was the fate of the sprog gunner, Slim, that they too had yet to hear from. Because you had simply made it out of an airborne bomber did not ensure your survival. There were myriad ways your fate could still be sealed.

"But I knew we'd be okay." Stan broke the contemplative silence. "I still had Percy with me." He broke into a wide grin and pulled out from his tunic pocket a small, stuffed penguin that he seemed to always carry with him on ops as a talisman. "'Percy the Penguin' has now become 'Percy the *Parachuting* Penguin'!"

They all laughed.

"How the hell did you get that past Jerry?" Len exclaimed. "The bastards even took my..." He paused, remembering at once both his confiscated blessed rosary and that he had always kept his deep faith secret from his crewmates. "My cigarettes." He finished, hoping that the lapse was untoward.

Stan simply shrugged. "Dunno. I reckon they didn't see it as a threat."

"A threat?" Hale said quickly. "They were laughing their arses off at 'im!"

"G'out!" Stan said earnestly. "It got us all here, di'n't it?" He carefully tucked the toy back in his pocket with all due reverence, as if it might be offended by this undeserved mocking.

The banter continued as they all found a place to again sit. If you took away the dark, cold room and locked door, they could almost be back in the ready room waiting to go on ops. Len's earlier apprehension was relieved somewhat by being with his crewmates. But he was still captive, with several of his closest friends absent. He had no idea what to expect from all this. After settling into the routine of operational flying—the always anxious if not downright terrifying routine of flying within heavy bombers over enemy territory—now he faced a future that he had not even contemplated. Where the hell was he? Where would he be taken? His heartbeat began to quicken with the uncertainty, so he tried pick up on the conversation from which he had withdrawn.

Stan beckoned the others to lean in close. "Reckon Robbie and Lofty made it?" he whispered. He was the first to reopen the subject of their missing compatriots since they had been brought together. Len knew that it had been on everyone's mind, but no one had dared say anything—either in fear of their captors overhearing or worse, considering that their friends were gone forever. The question hung in the air as each of them either shrugged or widened their eyes in resigned ignorance of what might have happened after each of them had bailed out. Left unspoken was their collective fervent wish for the best outcome.

"I jumped after Slim, and Pappy was coming right after, I'm dead sure," Len offered hopefully. He didn't want to embarrass Stan for not mentioning them in his earlier query, but he wanted to make certain that the other two who were still absent were included in their thoughts.

Len's comment seemed to shift their focus. It was Hale who turned on Len now and with facetious indignation asked, "What the hell happened back there? You spoiled an otherwise good prang with that flak shell you attracted." He was smiling throughout his accusation. "Are you okay?" Despite his offhand manner, Len could tell he was genuinely concerned.

"Yeah, I'm tickety-boo," Len said with manufactured conviction. He resisted the urge to flex his arms and legs, since every time he did, it sent sharp pangs through his perforated limbs. "But it made a ruddy mess of my turret. I just got the hell out of there before the bugger fell off the kite!" He laughed weakly while Hale shook his head in awe.

Wilkie chimed in with the assessment of the damage that he saw when he went to check on the welfare of the gunners near the rear of the airplane. "The turret was blown to bits—there wasn't even Perspex left! The port empennage was badly damaged from what I could make out." Len noticed the almost incongruous formal use of the term that collectively described all the control surfaces on the twin rudders of the Mark III Halifax they were flying. He'd have just called it the tail.

The initial excitement of knowing that some of his crewmates were alive and well was now wearing off as Len began to ponder the fate of the other men. The fact was that he was running largely on adrenaline and hadn't slept in over twenty-four hours, despite his fitful nap earlier. It was starting to take its toll on him as it seemed to be affecting the rest. They fell into an anxious silence.

There seemed to be some shouting in the hallway outside the door, and all four pricked up their ears. The locked door rattled again, and Len craned to see what surprise might transpire this time. The door was pushed open abruptly, and this time, a blue-uniformed airman was obviously shoved into the cell. The man faced back toward those whom had deposited him, but he stood still and drew his wiry frame to a dignified pose and with some élan, defiantly straightened his tunic. Even from behind, Len recognized the far from regulation length of the mop of hair on the man's head.

Pappy!

Stan and Hale were already moving toward him as Len struggled to stand against the pain in his shins. All pretense of feigning a lack of recognition was gone as the three rushed over to greet their irrepressible navigator.

"Where 'n hell had you gotten to?" It was Hale again with his show of mock anger at Pappy's late arrival.

Pappy simply shrugged. "At the pub, where else?" His teeth shone through his crooked smile.

"Yer off yer chump!" Stan physically took a step back as if trying to stave off catching whatever might be making Pappy this delusional. His wide grin, however, revealed just how happy he was to see the navigator.

Pappy held up his hand as if in testimony. "As God is my witness, I came down nice as can be and went to a farmhouse. This bird answers the door and after much hopping, swanning about, and charades, I finally convinced 'er to get help. Then the bint runs to the police!" He slapped his forehead and shook his head.

"But I guess she figured I looked like I needed a drink, so she drags me to this pub. Of course, it ain't open, but everyone in town comes by to have a peek. So I flashed my wad of dough and told the keep that the drinks were on me." Pappy paused for the anticipated reaction from those who knew him best and then he cackled. "Damned if I was gonna let Jerry have the lot!"

"What a line shoot!" It was all that Len could say in response, but the obvious lack of conviction in his accusation elicited only a playful slap on the shoulder. Len knew from reputation and experience that it was all true. He looked at his fellow Canadian and just knew that the Dutch would be telling, for years to come, how the RCAF airman parachuted into their town just to buy them all drinks.

"But the entire lot of them scattered like pigeons when the cops came to get me." Pappy just shook his head again. "Wasn't too bad, until the krauts discovered I was a Jew." There was an uncomfortable silence. Perhaps someone like Wilkie might perceive the muted reaction as the rest being uncomfortable with Pappy's ethnicity. Len knew that Stan and Hale were only contemplating what fate might befall their cherished crewmate in Nazi hands. It made Len nervous too.

Pappy tried to shift the focus. "Where's the skipper and the rest?" It was an unwise gambit, for the silence only grew more deafening. If Pappy could ever be contrite, Len figured this was how it looked.

He tried another tack. "When we getting out of this joint? I gotta bird in Brid I'm gonna get on with tonight." This broke the tension as they all laughed at that one.

"Robbie got me to send in the clear that we were bailing out over Holland," Hale reported. This was news to Len. It is little wonder that they were rounded up so quickly if the whole world was listening! "I'm sure the chaps back at base will take care of that skirt for you."

There was more laughter. Len's mood was lightened, at least for the moment. It was almost like being back at Lissett. The laughter must have drawn the attention of their captors, as the panel in the locked door slid open again. An eye appeared for a few seconds as it surveyed the interior. It disappeared to be replaced by a pair of lips that suddenly parted, issuing a foul gob in the direction of the cluster of airmen.

"Bloody 'ell!" exclaimed Hale as the bolus landed nearest him, but they all recoiled from the spittle. It was a sharp reminder that they were not in friendly hands.

The knot of airmen, most still sporting some accoutrements of flying kit, quickly sidled to the farthest wall. This was surely out of reach of even the longest spew. Len took the opportunity to sit on the makeshift bed. His leg wounds were aching, and he was quite suddenly very exhausted. It suddenly occurred to him that he ought to be very hungry as well, since his last full meal was more than twenty-four hours ago. He did not eat the pre-flight treat of an egg because he, along with the others, was certain that as a reserve crew, they would not be flying. He had planned to buy a proper meal in whatever town he first encountered today, the supposed first day of his leave. *Some leave!*

His contemplation had caused him to lose track of the continued excited conversation of his crewmates. They seemed to be trying to piece together what had happened to their bomber and to each of them during this sortie. At the best of times, operational flying was a tapestry of disparate events, tasks, and occurrences. Having your aircraft shot up and then flown in a crippled state for four hours only to end with a desperate parachute escape would require careful analysis to ever determine what had truly transpired. What was occurring in front of Len could not be classified as a debriefing.

"Lucky thing Robbie turned back from the sea, or we'd all have gone for the chop," Stan remarked rather casually. Certainly, having to bail out over or ditch into the cold, dark, windswept waters of the North Sea would have meant an uncertain future for them all. If the dinghy on the Halifax meant for a water landing had been damaged by the attacks, their chances might have been nil.

"Yer arse is a star!" Pappy countered immediately. "We were never over the drink. Robbie asked for a direct course back to base and that's what he was flying." As the crew's navigator, Pappy ought to know this.

"We never turned," Wilkie confirmed. As the second pilot he would have had a pretty good idea of this too, from helping Robbie fly the kite.

"From my seat, we were over water, and it looked pretty rough," Stan insisted. The clear Perspex nose of the air bomber's position would have given him a pretty good view. Len alternately envied and abjured the view up front in the Halifax for the vantage must be either breathtaking or terrifying.

"It was probably the Ems that you saw." Pappy seemed to have toned down his argument, trying to come up with a mollifying explanation for Stan's claim. Len could offer no opinion on this, since he was without benefit of a view after he had abandoned his rear turret and taken refuge amidships. Not that he was cognizant of much with his injuries and prolonged oxygen deprivation. All he could recall was the slap-happy banter he and the now-absent Lofty had exchanged while sharing their one oxygen mask.

"Well, maybe …" Stan conceded. But to Len's ear, he sounded unconvinced. As pieces of their flight's puzzle were revealed, there were things that

Len could fit into a reasonable explanation. There were others that he could not. All he knew was what had happened to him, and even of that he was far from certain.

One thing was clear in Len's mind: their skipper had done a wizard job of getting them as far as he had. Here were five men who might not have been alive if not for his skill and determination. The image of Robbie's steely concentration and vise-like grip on the control column of the bomber was etched in his mind. It was always said that the rear gunner in the bomber had the most dangerous seat, but it was always the pilot whose sworn duty it was to make certain all his charges had the best chance to exit the airplane. In another time, Robbie would have been written up in the *London Gazette* for his actions. But it was ever thus for aircrew in Bomber Command. You only ever got a "gong" if there were witnesses to your feat. For the myriad heroic activities that took place each night from a multitude of crews, there were seldom survivors to give testimony. And very few survivors would ever shoot such a line in any case.

Some time had passed in relative silence while the lucky five exchanged sporadic snippets and contemplated their relative good fortune but uncertain future. To no one's surprise, Pappy curled up on the stiff wooden shelf and was soon snoring so loudly that the rest moved to quieter confines.

"Thank goodness I've never shared quarters with that," Len said, motioning to the obliviously somnolent navigator, whose stentorian snuffling had even caused their German captors to peek inside the cell once again.

"Tell me about it!" Stan, the only other commissioned rank in the group, chimed in. "If I had the cotton batting concession in our hut, I'd be a rich man!"

They all laughed but then fell into relative quiet again. Len thought he heard something outside the cell, so turned his attention to the door once again. The now familiar sound of the keys rattling in the lock caused his heartbeat to quicken once again. Every time that door had opened it brought good news and so conditioned, Len had already begun to rise. The others had not had his run of fortune with crewmates joining their cadre and seemed somewhat less anxious.

Through the now opened door came two more men—one leading the way while the shorter of the two walked a respectful pace behind. Their clothes were muddy and wet, but their faces instantly lit up in recognition.

"Wotcher!" Lofty nearly shouted as he entered the cell behind Robbie. The door again slammed behind them. Wilkie and Hale joined Len in jumping up to meet them. Stan shook their sleeping companion, shouting, "Pappy! Wake up! Skipper's here!"

The seven men met near the centre of the cell. The room that had been so dark, gloomy, and empty when Len first entered hours ago was now as raucous as the sergeants' mess on a dance night. Everyone had smiles plastered to their faces in abject joy. Robbie seemed happy and appeared as if a heavy weight had been lifted from his shoulders.

During the ruckus, the door panel slid open once again. This time, several gobs issued forth in rapid succession. Luckily, the newcomers had been ushered out of projectile range by those whom had already suffered this indignity. It seemed clear that the good cheer of the captives was more than unpalatable to those on the outside.

"Where's Slim?" Robbie asked, as his light mood seemed to darken. There were several shrugs of uncertainty as the skipper's inquisitive, expectant gaze fell on each one in turn. When he got to Len, it was he who finally spoke.

"I went out just after him, but I never saw any chutes. Jerry must have seen me come down, 'cos they picked me up as I landed." Len shook his head, as he could offer no more information. They all knew what was most likely. It was probable that he had a bad trip out, a parachute that didn't deploy properly, or he didn't survive landing. There was a chance that he might still be picked up—and an even slimmer chance that he was evading capture. In any case, little more needed to be said. Robbie seemed disappointed in the news, but Len hoped he took solace in seeing most of his crew relatively safe and sound in front of him.

When the back-slapping and greeting died down, it was Pappy who broached the subject of the newcomers' dishevelled appearance.

"What the hell happened to you two? You look like you were dragged through a hedge backwards!" Pappy indicated the muck covering their lower legs and smeared across various areas of their uniform. "Did you bail out into a swamp?"

"Just our idea of disguise," Robbie said simply as he looked down at his muddied attire, looking somewhat abashed.

Lofty took off from that. "Skip put the kite down in a field! It was his least ropey landing ever." He smiled while delivering that jibe. "I was back o' the main spar and didn't even feel us touch!"

"Come on! Pull the other one!" Hale said in what might have been sincere disbelief, but Lofty nodded in enthusiastic response while Robbie just shrugged. This was as much confirmation as Len and the others needed. If any pilot could bring a stricken four-engine bomber down safely, it was their captain.

As if to ward off any kudos, Robbie turned quite serious. "We tried to torch the kite, but someone's pinched the incendiary." His eyes shifted from man to man as if searching for a culprit.

After an uncomfortable moment, Pappy said meekly, "I hear those things fetch a couple bob in town …" He trailed off with a supplicating palm turned upwards. But Robbie's point was made. He had put the Halifax down to save himself and his engineer, but now there it stood, unbroken, to be pored over by the enemy. He turned silently and walked to the corner to sit. Only Wilkie followed, as if in solidarity of pilots who shared the leadership and responsibility for their crews and aircraft.

Lofty waited until his captain was on the other side of the room before he started talking in a voice scarcely above a whisper.

"Robbie was wizzo! When I went to get our chutes, mine was shot through—NBG! When I told him, he insisted it was his!" Lofty paused, but not one of his five crewmates expressed any surprise. "So after I do a quick check to see all of yeh have gone, 'e says he's gonna put the kite down. Just like that!"

Len listened intently to the excited engineer. The question briefly occurred to him that if one of the parachutes was still serviceable, why hadn't Lofty used it? But he knew in an instant from spending so much time with this crew, in the air and on the ground, that loyalty trumped all. Indeed, Len now felt vaguely guilty that he, himself, had abandoned the aircraft.

"So I do what I can with the throttles and juice when he finally tells me to go back to the spar and brace myself. I no sooner get there, lookin' fer the best place t'be, and he shows up behind me! I figure, 'Bloody 'ell, who's flying this!' And he says, 'we're down'."

"So we tried to light a fire and then scrambled out the top hatch. We had a quick squint 'round the kite. It was in decent shape, 'cept for the arse end." Lofty paused and looked straight at Len. "Are you sure you're okay, mate? Your seat looks like Swiss cheese!"

"Doin' okay," Len said with mustered conviction. They had all been through a turn. He honestly felt that his performance in the matter was the least heroic of any of them. He certainly was not going to invite untoward attention.

Lofty continued to talk of their abortive attempt to elude capture, but Len felt he needed to sit once again. He moved near to where Robbie and Wilkie were comparing their stories and then he sat on the floor. The two paused briefly as if to welcome his participation, but when he made no overture, they continued their conversation without him.

Len stared blankly across the cell at the locked door. The panel occasionally slid open as he watched and waited. There was no more spitting. Their German captors seemed content to just observe.

Len waited anxiously for the glorious sound of the locked portal opening one more time, for it might presage the arrival of their last missing crew member, the replacement mid-upper turret gunner. A bomber crew numbered seven, and perhaps after filling their cell with that many, Jerry would stop looking. It could be that Slim now had a good chance of getting away. That would certainly be best. But maybe the next best thing would be to have that door open again. And maybe it wasn't entirely a bad thing to associate a closed door with hope.

13

The living room chesterfield stood at a perverse angle with one end about a foot higher on some makeshift prop of my father's design. On the couch he was prostrate with his head at the lower end. Under his chest was a piece of plywood that, when not providing a solid underpinning for this event, fit neatly tucked beneath our furniture. Beside him, within easy reach, was a box of tissue and a garbage can he had borrowed from the bedroom. This scene was commonplace in our home and would often be repeated several times a week.

My mother, her hands cupped, was rhythmically striking Dad's middle to upper back and ribs. My eldest sister waited her turn to take over from Mom when she tired. At regular intervals, Dad would cough rather productively and expectorate into a waiting tissue that he would then neatly fold and place in the container provided. I was to learn years later that this was called "chest percussions" and is often prescribed for those with excess mucous in their lungs. We all called it simply "pounding Daddy's back."

I sidled closer; after all, this was a family activity. I was certain that all families gathered around their father routinely to pound his chest. My mother paused and wiped her forehead with the back of her hand while Dad coughed deeply and carefully expelled a bolus of phlegm into another tissue, and it too went into the garbage. Mom then motioned for my sister to continue.

"I want a turn!" I blurted out. Mother sighed while my sister just looked at me with some exasperation.

"Okay, Son," Dad intoned, and I enthusiastically leapt to the task. I pounded with the gusto I had seen my mother and siblings employ. There was, however, not a lot of strength in my seven-year-old arms, and it was clear that my efforts were never near as efficacious as what he required, plus I was tuckered out in less than thirty seconds.

"Did I do good, Daddy?"

Dad pulled another tissue from the box, drew a very deep breath, and forced a cough from his raspy lungs. He made a great show of spitting something into the white paper and then showed it to me. It was a tiny bit of phlegm. He disposed of it like the others.

"Thank you, Son," he said simply and then added, "Good job."

My sister started her duty as Mom stood by with an all-too-familiar look of concern on her face. Largely oblivious to all this, I turned away, satisfied with my contribution. The clap of cupped hand against bare flesh echoed easily off our largely bare, wood-grain panelled walls, and so filled our house with a vital, comforting beat. I wandered off to whatever else I might find to occupy my evening.

Len sat on the edge of what passed for a bed in the dismal open ward of the prison camp's infirmary. His shoulders were hunched into one of the few positions that minimized the pain in his right chest that seemed to accompany every breath. His bare legs protruded from his hospital gown. His feet were covered in the oft-darned socks that provided some small comfort from the decidedly slipshod environment that *Stalag Luft IV's* sick quarters provided for those prisoners fortunate enough to be granted space.

This stooped posture necessarily focussed his attention on his lower legs. He appraised each in turn and noted how the scars from his injuries had healed quite nicely. The wounds were all neatly covered with fresh, pink skin. It was a far cry from the oozing red sores from which he had picked and gouged a variety of sharp shards of metal that had been imbedded in his legs when the flak shell had exploded beneath his turret. He had been pleased with the treatment he had given himself in this matter. At the time, the last thing he would have done was to accept any assistance from his German captors.

But now here he was—beholden to Jerry after all, as were the scores of other *kriegies* being kept here in a variety of states of health. He was not as bad off as many of the others in the ward, but the state of his health had ebbed and flowed over the time he had been ensconced here. How long had it been? It was part of his daily routine to calculate the exact length of his hospitalization. It was now October 26, and he first came to the infirmary on the last day of August. That made it …

Len's hands were in his lap as he started sticking digits into the air as he counted silently to himself. He already knew what number he'd come up with, for it was the same number he came up with this morning and one less than he'd arrive at tomorrow. Counting gave him something to do and often calmed him. There was something elemental in the tally. Sometimes he would count in French just for some variety. He suspected that through sheer assimilation that he could even perform the task in German, but the mere thought filled him with revulsion.

"What d'ya come up with this time?" said the emaciated man in the next bunk. Len peered at him from under his knitted brows without lifting his head. The tone was facetious, but there was no hint of a smile on the man's lips.

Len had dealt with every sort of character through his military service and now through his nearly nine months in enemy incarceration. Staying on the good side of folks only took patience and understanding, and if that failed, he found that stony silence was often a viable option. He need not have worried.

"Fifty-six days, Eddie," he replied evenly and then added after a thoughtful pause, "I guess that makes it seventy-nine for you."

Eddie only grunted. It was a wonder he had the strength to do that. The American had been a waist gunner on a B-17 that had been shot down by an FW 190 early in 1944. He had been part of the brutal trip from *Stalag Luft VI* in Heydekrug to their current internment here in Gross Tychow. Len didn't even want to think of that journey, which seemed to progress from indignity to inhumanity. It went from them herded into overloaded railway cattle cars to being entombed in the hold of a near-derelict freight ship—all the while with no food, water, or sanitation. Few of them thought they would survive, but to a man, they seemed to tap a well of resolve that they would not be broken. The last few miles were the worst. It was a sprint while handcuffed to another prisoner through a gauntlet of fixed bayonets and guard dogs. That's where they got Eddie.

Len managed to avoid major injury during this free-for-all, but only because he had heeded the rifle shots being fired at those too weak or recalcitrant to double time it to the new *Stalag's* gates. Eddie, along with several others, were jabbed and sliced with bayonets or bludgeoned with rifle butts. And like the others, Eddie steadfastly refused to have even admitted that the brutal treatment had done any harm. That was until the infection had set in to several of the punctures, necessitating his hospitalization.

But Len had had his own problems. The massive fever that accompanied the acute pain and difficulty breathing had him almost delirious when he was first brought to the infirmary. Eddie was there then, and Len dimly remembered the gaunt man giving words of encouragement. The phrase that stuck out during even the most confused times was, "Don't let the Kraut bastards win."

He did not. Somehow, the Allied doctors who were also prisoners had convinced the lone German physician who was responsible for the care of thousands of prisoners to treat Len with a course of sulpha-based antibiotics. It took several days, but the infection and fever seemed to subside, even if the pain and breathing problems persisted. Antibiotics did not seem to help Eddie, however, and it appeared that the weeping wounds that he still bore would never heal. It didn't help either of them that despite their hospitalization, they were still on meagre rations that left them both malnourished and underfed. Len was probably lucky that he had had the constitution of a horse before the war and through his service. Eddie looked like he'd had a sallow cast all his life.

"I wonder if *Herr Doktor* will be by today," Eddie said finally, and coughed deeply. Len wished he hadn't, for the primal urge to emulate, he knew, would throw his lungs into a paroxysm. Another shallow inhalation seemed to quell the instinct.

Doctor Sommer was the chief and only German medical officer assigned to look after the needs of the Allied POWs. His neatly coifed hair was greying at the temples and his immaculately kept uniform was in stark contrast to every other man in the hospital. Even the guards and orderlies paled in comparison. He made infrequent rounds of the sick here. He'd look at each man's skimpy chart, jot an occasional note, and then move on, seldom saying a word. Len thought for a while that he might not speak English, but after the bitter tirade he launched one day when another patient had said some uncomplimentary things within his earshot, it was clear that he was at least conversant enough to understand insults.

The Allied doctors had repeatedly suggested to Sommer that both Len and Eddie, along with several others, ought to be turned over to neutral or Allied care. It was with mixed feelings that Len reacted to the friendly doctors examining him. Their grim faces as they listened to his rattily breathing told him more than he wanted to know. But their pleading that he should be turned loose gave him a faint hope that he might see his family, or even the outside world, once more. Alas, it was ultimately up to the taciturn enemy *Doktor* to make that decision, and he had refused each entreaty.

And so he waited. What else was there to do but languish? In his darker moments, Len would wonder if death was not preferable. When he was captured, he expected the loss of freedom. He had even anticipated some mistreatment or physical hardship. But he had not even imagined how the absence of so many things he had taken for granted would gnaw at him—a glass of cold milk, the song of a meadowlark, the dancing hues of a prairie sunset, or the soft comfort of a woman—any woman. Deprived of almost everything that made one human, would not the succor of a promised eternal reward be the better choice? But he had built up so much hate for this captivity and those who administered it that he knew he would not be forgiven now. He must survive until his death might be on his own terms.

Len's introspection was interrupted by some silent yet fervent gestures from Eddie. The purposeful, repeated toss of his head drew attention to the much-anticipated visit by the Allied prisoner doctor on his rounds with Dr. Sommer. They were moving quickly from bed to bed with very little communication between them. The German would pause at each patient and write some notes, occasionally using a stethoscope to listen to a chest or gesturing to the POW doctor to pull back a dressing to examine a wound or other ailing body part.

The pair made their way to where Len and Eddie's gurneys were parked. With them were a German orderly and the ever-present Luftwaffe prison guard. The goon was rather slovenly, especially when compared to the dapper Sommer. He did, however, sport the disdainful sneer that seemed ubiquitous on these sorts, as if their lot somehow compared to that of those they were holding captive. Len did not know the American army doctor's name. He did not have a nameplate but wore the rank insignia of a captain. Everyone simply called him "Doc," and he answered to the same.

They first stopped by Eddie, and Sommer stood a cautious distance back from the bed while Doc lay bare what were likely the worst of Eddie's infections. The German peered briefly at what he'd been shown and inscrutably shook his head fractionally while simultaneously raising his clipboard and scribbling something. Len saw Doc put a comforting hand on Eddie's shoulder and may have even smiled, for the patient nodded in response. The scene, bereft of any compassion by their captors, played out wordlessly in a manner that was incongruous to any dealings Len had ever known with medics before his capture. Unfortunately, it was all too familiar in his experience here.

The pair turned to Len. Sommer flipped his clipboard to a new page and briefly examined it. He handed the chart to Doc and then put his stethoscope into his ears while roughly pulling back the gown covering Len's back. The cold metal of the instrument gave Len a start, but he fought what would have been a painful inhalation.

"*Atme!*" the German commanded. Len looked questioningly at Doc.

"Breathe," the friendly American translated. Len inhaled to the point of intense pain in his right upper quadrant and then breathed out slowly.

"*Tief einatmen!*" Sommer said impatiently.

"As deep as you can," Doc added. Len steeled himself and then inhaled as much as he could chance. It caught in his chest as he struggled to expel it evenly. He repeated this twice more with the same excruciating result. It felt like there was a steel band across his chest and it cut him deeply—not just when he breathed in but almost as badly when he let it go.

Sommer whipped the stethoscope from his ears and snatched the clipboard back from Doc who gestured to the paper and shook his head slightly while giving a slight shrug of his shoulders. Sommer again scribbled something, and the entourage moved on.

It took several minutes of careful, slow breaths before Len could do so with only the familiar dull ache he had been living with for at least six weeks. By this time, Sommer was out of earshot, so Eddie chanced a critique of their most recent encounter.

"Same bushwa every time," Eddie said in a tone that sounded close to despair. "They can't look after us decent, but they won't send us back. What the hell threat are we to anyone? I am so weak, I can barely stand, and you don't have the wind to get to the latrine!"

Len was not moved to respond in any fashion to this outburst. He decided that he would save his energy for something that mattered. Yes, he was weary. He was frustrated. He was despondent. But Eddie's tirade seemed only to prove which of them was in worse shape. He let the silence lengthen between them.

In time, the ward returned to the dull murmur that had become commonplace. Few talked; many sighed, coughed, grunted, or moaned. The occasional shuffling of someone moving in their crude bed space brought to mind the sameness of life outside the hospital walls, in the barracks huts where Len's mates, friends, and compatriots—fellow POWs—also languished. The only sound that made this different was the near-constant clacking of the German orderlies on their typewriters. Overall, the dull drone was strangely comforting.

Len sighed as deeply as he dared and moved to his meagre kit. Maybe, he reckoned, if he tried to dress in what passed for his normal clothes, he might feel better. He pulled on his near-threadbare trousers and shirt. The shoes were scuffed and worn, each lace was knotted several times where they had broken, but when aligned properly in their military precision they gave him a vague remembrance of soldierly order. He stood briefly for a moment to the full height his emaciated and pain-ravaged body could muster. It reminded him of normalcy and the pride that duty and purpose engendered. But there was no parade to attend, so he slowly sat on his gurney once more.

"Going somewhere?" Eddie chided. Len managed a wan smile in response. He knew that Eddie wasn't being unkind. It was just his manner. Len knew full well that neither had chosen this fate. They were in it together, and nothing was likely to change that. Eddie was not the sort of character with whom Len would normally choose to spend time; however, deprivation of freedom, food, health, dignity, and even decency cut to the core and formed a bond that few on the outside could ever understand. There was little point in replying substantially to Eddie's comment, so Len just let it drop. So many conversations in the past few months seemed to start and end this way.

Without a lot of warning, a curtain parted at the far end of the hut that was their hospital ward. It was there to give a small measure of separation between the medical staff and their captive patients. Through the opening emerged two German orderlies and Doc and they strode purposely toward Len and Eddie. The look on Doc's face was very hard to read, but if Len had to guess, it was somewhere between satisfaction and consternation. Len stood as they approached.

"We thought you might like to see this," Doc said as he handed over a neatly stapled clutch of papers. Len glanced at them but it all made little sense to him. The pages were written in German, but from what he knew, it seemed to be his medical chart. He could make out his name and prisoner number, 1015. Along one side were dates with details written in an adjacent column. What did it all mean? Was it bad news? Was he as sicker than he thought?

Near the bottom of the page, Len could make out Doc's signature and today's date. Above that was written in German, "*Die Heimkehrberechtigung wird bejaht—verneint.*" The last word had a line drawn neatly through it. It meant nothing to him. He flipped to the next page but found only more typewritten German, ending with what he knew to be Dr. Sommer's signature. He flipped the sheaf closed again and handed back to the now widely grinning doctor.

"It says you can go home."

Len stood staring. Doc then turned to meet Eddie's expectant gaze and cast down his eyes while slowly shaking his head. No words were needed. He then turned back toward Len, still standing dumbstruck, and slowly repeated, "You … can … go … home."

Len snatched the papers back into his own hand and thrust it high in the air while letting out a thunderous "Whoop!"

"Lucky shit ..." Len heard Eddie mutter from behind Doc and the German orderlies.

"When? ... How?" Len babbled.

"You are to assemble in the *Vorlager* by sixteen-hundred. There's about two dozen of you. You'll be turned over to the Red Cross and then it's likely on to Switzerland."

Len looked at the clock on the wall. It was just after 1300.

"Geez, I gotta go," he said, and he vaulted over his bed to where his kit was stored and quickly started shoving things into his rucksack. Len noticed in mid-leap that the Germans who had accompanied Doc actually took a step back and cast an astonished glance at each other. Len wondered if they might reconsider his apparent ill state, but frankly did not care what they thought. He had his freedom clutched firmly in his hand. The pain in his chest was excruciating—probably as bad or worse than almost anything he'd felt. But he wasn't going to show it. He might collapse a yard outside of the *Stalag*, but at least it would be outside.

He hastily assembled the few belongings he had here and then paused between his bed and Eddie's. He looked at the despondent man in the next bed and tried to find words. He was over the moon at his own release, but now he stood staring into the unreadable eyes of the man who would be left behind. Words failed to come.

"Get the hell out of here," Eddie finally said with a sincere grin on his face. The sudden appearance of blacked and nutritionally ravaged teeth made Len realize that Eddie had never bared them before. He shuffled his load to free his hand to offer a hearty handshake and then he quickly made for the door. He strode past Doc and the orderlies giving another man the news that he was going home. It seemed that Len's earlier euphoric outburst now had the entire room on tenterhooks, so they largely ignored him as he rushed past.

Len passed several guards and other personnel, holding his papers in front of him like a carte blanche. When he finally exited the building, he squinted against the bright yet cloudy sky. It was chilly, even for late October, and in his illness-weakened state, his tunic was barely sufficient against the damp cold. But he needed to get to his hut to collect what he could there and say goodbye to his mates. He also needed to find Robbie, Lofty, and Hale, who were in another barracks. There was no way he could leave without seeing his crewmates after all they had been through together.

There wasn't much left of his possessions in his old hut. The space was now occupied and his larder scattered. Had he been coming back to stay, there might have been hell to pay. Even the faces did not seem familiar, what with the constant influx of newly arrived captive airmen joining their ranks every day. He noticed that the previously double-decked bunks were now organized into three tiers, so the barracks was even more crammed than he had previously known. The denizens were a motley collection of mostly Canadians, but with airmen from the Commonwealth well-represented.

Len's arrival elicited blank stares from most of those assembled. He searched for a familiar face and finally settled on his old friend and protector, Stu. It seemed that captivity was taking its toll on Stu. While he once cut an imposing figure, the man was now pallid and drawn.

"Stu, I'm going home," Len said evenly, not sure what reaction this might provoke among those still trapped here. "I wanted to say goodbye. Do you know where Nick is?"

Stu looked back at him for a long moment. Len saw several emotions run fleetingly across the man's face, almost too quickly to fully discern. There was surprise, envy, happiness, longing, anger, and several more that defied description. With what might have been tears welling in the big man's eyes, he shook his head slowly. Len was running strictly on emotional energy by now, but knew that he, himself, must look even more frail and unwell than those he was speaking to. He looked at Stu quizzically and finally, under the lengthening stare, the big man wordlessly tossed his head in the direction of a knot of *kriegies* in the far corner.

"Thank you," Len said automatically and then added without thinking, "See you," as he turned to find Nick. He did not look back, but he felt several pairs of eyes burning into his back.

Len approached the clutch of RCAF prisoners gathered around a bunk. Nick's easy manner was easy to pick out, even from a distance. Len approached slowly to not repeat the awkwardness that the meeting with Stu created, but Nick saw him first and jumped to his feet.

"Geez, Len, you look like a sack of shit tied in the middle!" Nick always had a way with words. "What's up?"

"Jerry's released me to the Red Cross. I'm outta here in about an hour," Len offered cautiously.

In sharp contrast to the earlier encounter, Nick and his companions started patting Len on the back and celebrating. A couple of the blokes made crude jokes about catching whatever illness Len had to lead to this. Len didn't correct them. He took it in the spirit intended, even if he wouldn't have wished this ordeal on anyone.

"I'm fighting the clock a little here, Nick," Len said finally, "but I couldn't leave without saying goodbye. I still need to find my boys."

"Of course," Nick said softly. He knew full well that Len was referring to his crewmates in the RAF hut next door. Few bonds were that strong. "We'll be right on your tail, soon, I am sure. You take care of yourself."

The two long-time brothers-in-arms embraced meaningfully. It was a bit of a shock to Len, since their previous intimacy was limited to an occasional handshake. But it was extraordinary circumstances, so Len thought it was more than appropriate. He turned to leave without a backward glance.

In the adjoining hut, Len found his captured crewmates quite easily. It was always Robbie, Lofty, and Hale together as if they had always been that way and always would. Sometimes Len wondered how there might still be anything to talk about, but then realized that so much of such a bond was wordless. He had gotten over the guilt he initially felt by leaving their company during the early days of their incarceration here. In their frequent encounters since, not one of them displayed any suggestion that they felt that they had been abandoned. Len knew implicitly that his move to be with the other Canadian *kriegies* was accepted. After all, Wilkie, who was with them when they were shot down, had joined a different cohort before Len had gone his own way.

It was Hale who saw Len approaching first, and his gentle nudge in the ribs of Robbie and Lofty had them all standing and grinning widely as their mate approached.

"So they finally sprung you from sick call," said Robbie as he thrust out a welcoming hand.

"Hang on to your hat," Len said, barely containing his ecstasy which now, having told enough people, was tinged with bewilderment, "I'm going home!"

The three Englishmen looked him up and down with mouths agape. Finally, it was Lofty who exclaimed, "Bloody 'ell, Len! Are you barmy? You ain't gone wire-happy, 'ave ya? How the … what the …" He trailed off sputtering.

Robbie was left speechless, still holding Len's hand. He raised a quizzical eyebrow to his friend and former tail gunner. Len just met his questioning look with a rapid and repeated definitive nod. Robbie started shaking his hand even more enthusiastically. Hale stood quietly behind his pilot and the faithful flight engineer. He seemed to be muttering to himself. Len thought he saw the crew's wireless operator's eyes starting to grow misty.

Before things turned too maudlin, Hale jumped to the fore and started pounding Len on the back. "We've gotta have a piss up. I can scare up some d-bars, biscuits, and tinned sausages. We gonna send y'off proper." The other two seemed in full agreement.

"Uh, no can do, mates. Doc said we're leavin' from the *vorlager* at sixteen-hundred."

"We?" Lofty asked. "How many?"

"Twenty or so," Len said with a shrug, "I dunno. I didn't stick around for all the details. When they gave me my papers, I bolted like a scalded cat before they changed their minds." Len paused for effect. "I think the Jerries were a little surprised when I jumped over the bed on my way out!"

They all laughed.

"Where are they sending you?" Lofty asked.

"I really don't know, sorry," Len shook his head slowly. "I'm assuming it'll be to the Red Cross, and then who knows …"

"If you're back in Blighty, get word to m'folks, ok?" Now Robbie was welling up as he added. "You know where to find them."

"Mine, too!" Lofty and Hale chimed in near unison.

Len looked at each in turn as he spoke. "You know I will."

Robbie looked at his watch as if to keep the scene from getting too emotional. He said brightly as he clasped an arm around his soon-to-be homeward-bound friend, "We'll walk you as far as permitted."

Len walked with his crew one last time toward the end of the camp where the gates had first closed behind them. Silence hung in the air as the mates moved slowly together as they had so many times before. Their shared service and sacrifice bred brotherhood that had rendered words largely superfluous. But it still seemed that something should be said.

Len looked out to the distance where life over the wire might truly still exist and said to no one in particular, "I cannot help thinking of the Vera Lynn song …"

Robbie stopped and waited until Len finally paused, turned, and looked back at him. "You know, mate, I was having the very same thought." And he started to laugh. On either side of him, Lofty and Hale threw arms around their skipper's shoulders and started an off-key rendition.

"We'll meet again. Don't know where … Don't know when. But I know we'll meet again some sunny day …"

Len just slowly shook his head and took one last lingering look at the three of them. He turned and continued walking toward the knot of official-looking men gathered in the *Vorlager*. He could still hear them singing as he showed his papers to the goon guarding the last gate to his freedom.

14

It was Father's Day in 1967 and what a day it had been. The weather had been cloudy and cool all day, but the late sun of this near solstice period still had us frolicking until late. This Sunday, of course, had started with Mass and our usual "feast" at lunchtime. We gave Dad our gifts in the afternoon. Mine was rather modest—a card that each of us in our Grade 2 class had been tasked to make on the previous Friday. I thought it paled in comparison to the extravagance of my siblings, but he seemed to enjoy my efforts.

The balance of the afternoon was spent assembling the charcoal barbeque that my older brothers and sisters had chipped in to buy for my father. My eldest brother was no longer living at home, and his work at a local dairy, I assumed, had allowed him to be the major financial contributor to this new addition to our back yard. Most other houses in our neighbourhood already sported this accoutrement—it was a status symbol, the level of which could be discerned from the features of the unit. Ours was simple; the one "extra" was a hood that served to shelter the briquette pan. Only the more well-to-do families had ones with wheels or the ultimate—an electric rotisserie.

Dad was not especially gifted with skills of assembly. Indeed, most mechanical tasks were a struggle for him. It did not help that his suite of tools was frequently raided by his kids for whatever nefarious project we might undertake. Today he was reduced to working with a pair of slip-joint pliers and a butter knife pressed into service as a screwdriver. It had not gone well, and there had been a few interesting turns of phrase—including one of his favourites, cursing the contraption as "Jerry-built." I didn't understand the reference at the time; our neighbour's name was Jerry, but *his* barbeque was expertly assembled.

But that was this afternoon. I had not realized that Dad and my brothers had disappeared, because I was in the process of getting ready for bed; after all, I still had school the next day. Suddenly they all reappeared with several brown, wax paper-wrapped bundles in hand. They had been to our meat locker to pick up steaks and had also stopped at a service station to pick up charcoal briquettes and lighter fluid. Dad was not going to let the day's festivities end without christening his half-assembled Father's Day gift.

All normal routine seemed to be abandoned as my mother and older sisters began to throw together a meagre salad and boiled potatoes. My brothers set about trying to help Dad get the barbeque going, which seemed to entail copious amounts, if not all, of the lighter fluid. I was only eight years old, so I was not much use in any of the tasks. I was just happy to meander between each working group.

At one point, a brother took me aside and told me solemnly, "Dad is really mad that you are up so late on a school night."

I was devastated. I could not understand how Dad could feel this way, but it must be true: in a busy family our size, news of this sort was frequently delegated to intermediaries. I slowly turned to resume my bedtime chores and went to the bathroom.

Our bathroom looked out over the patio, and I could not resist climbing on the edge of the tub to peer out the window. There was Dad tending the still flaming barbeque. He had put the frozen steaks on the grill and was busy cajoling them to keep them out of the worse of the conflagration. I viewed this scene, from which I had been inexplicably banned, with tears streaming from my eyes and down my cheeks. The waves of heat, the pall of smoke, and my tear-brimmed eyes clouded the view.

Suddenly, Dad noticed his audience. His face brightened like I had rarely seen and while an enormous grin flashed, he gave me an exaggerated beckoning wave. I covered the short distance from bathroom to backyard in what must have been heroic time and stood beside him in the gathering twilight. I never knew what made my brother tell me what he did, but I will always remember the wonderful taste of those charred and kerosene infused steaks.

Len absently surveyed the desultory scene that threatened to envelope him. It was a mess. People were rushing around and shouting, and he would occasionally acknowledge their interruptions. He was trying to make sense out of the surrounding chaos. The smoke and flames mixed with the pungent petroleum scent only added to the surreal nature of the night. Yet he was strangely at peace with everything, especially with his youngest son here at his side.

This was no way to cook what was, for this family, an expensive cut of meat! But tonight, it seemed right. He would make it work. He owed this much to his family. He again prodded a large chunk of meat away from a rather recalcitrant flame with the ladle that he had fashioned into a barbeque utensil. He was intensely grateful for the day that his family had given him.

He had so many good things, and they all seemed to be here with him. He didn't know what the future held, but he had been warned many times by any number of doctors that he was living on borrowed time. He told that to no one, of course, especially not to his dear Molly. But she seems to know. She fusses so much about him, looking after him and worrying, it seems every minute, so much that he sometimes reckoned that if he was finally gone, her burden might be lessened. She would be devastated, as he would be without her, but she is strong. He knew that of her as well.

This family will be okay.

Yes, the kids are still young, but they are growing up so quickly and so well. They each seem to embody what he has always aspired to. They all seem marvellously gifted—artists and artisans, thinkers and dreamers, generous and compassionate, principled and moral. He doubted any of them would be rich, but that was not the way he raised them. He was proud of each and every one of them, for they were each blessed in some special way.

A turbulent eddy from the flame pan in front of him brought a waft of acrid smoke and kerosene to his nostrils. Smells always conjure deep memories and suddenly he was back, trussed up in his flying kit and hunched in the rear turret of a Halifax bomber. Robbie … or Barry, or Tom, or Dougie, or any of the other skippers he had flown with, had just started the engines. The exhaust of their four engines along with swirling fumes from spilled aviation fuel here on the hardstand assaulted his nose. He would soon be on his way from RAF Lissett to over enemy territory to defend his six dearest friends and crewmates from mortal opposition fire as they struck another blow against Nazi tyranny. He was vital and alive at this moment, but there was any number of ways that he might not live through this hour, night, or tour. He was prepared. All that mattered was that he was here with those with whom he was closest.

Len felt a tug on his hand and he looked down into the spectacled eyes of his son, still standing wordlessly beside him. He was pointing at one of the steaks on the barbeque that seemed to have, itself, caught fire. Len just smiled down at the slight lad and tousled his hair while patting at the charred gristle. Maybe it was a good thing that the boy would never know what he'd been thinking.

Molly appeared at the side door and inquired, "Len, are you ready?"

"Just about, Honey…" he replied while still squelching the last of the flares from the burnt edges of the meat. A sheepish grin played on his face. His dear wife only shook her head admonishingly but with obvious devotion. She handed him a plate and disappeared inside.

Len scooped up the still sputtering, blackened steaks from the grill with his ladle and said with a sigh, "Okay, Son, we're done here."

He made his way up the few steps into his home to his awaiting family. The boy dutifully followed.

EPILOGUE

My father, Leonard Elric Cote, died on December 12, 1967. He had entered hospital about two weeks before that, sick with what developed into pneumonia. After about a week into his hospital stay, and from multiple systems shutting down, he slipped into a coma from which he did not awaken.

His death was deemed to be a result of injuries he sustained during the mistreatment that he, along with so many others, had suffered during his period of internment in a German POW camp after his aircraft was shot down and he was captured in 1944. It was difficult for our family, but his loving wife, our mother, Julia Malvina "Molly" Cote, nee Szakacs, worked and fought hard for our survival. She did wonders with the small War Widow's Pension she received, along with the full time work she needed to undertake to support our still young family. My older siblings thought they might lose her, too; she was so devastated by Dad's death. But their strength and devotion allowed mother to get back on her feet and carry on what she and my father had begun. She is as much a hero as I judge my father to be—she even had a medal to prove it. She has the Memorial Cross owing to Dad's passing being a direct result of his wartime RCAF service.

Dad only flew thrice more after he was shot down. Twice, he recorded gleefully in his wartime logbook, as a "paying passenger" on civilian flights that must have been part of rather extravagant vacations before he was married. One was a return trip of 150 miles to Saskatoon from Regina, Saskatchewan. Another was from Helena, Montana to Lethbridge, Alberta. He happily added five hours of flying time to his totals. His last flight was return to Montreal from Regina for participation in a national union convention in the last month before his death. He was quite excited to fly at nearly twice the altitude he had ever previously achieved, and on a jet aircraft, no less! I still remember his tiny plastic replica of the newly-introduced DC-9 jetliner that all passengers were given after it came into Air Canada service in 1966.

While in Montreal, he also was able to visit some of the places venerated by his church. My mother always harboured a sneaking suspicion that his journey up the torturous steps of St. Joseph's Oratory contributed to the illness that led to his death only a few weeks later. I imagine, however, that he would not have been denied. Joseph was my father's third given name, and St. Joseph was his most revered saint and, not coincidentally, the patron of a happy death. That was, in the end, all that Dad had wished for.

I have always wanted to know more about my father and was especially fascinated by his decisions in early adulthood to join a fight that many could argue was not his. At the same time, I have sometimes felt cheated that he left us so early, before I could ask questions that he might have not even chosen to answer. We all knew that he was in the war, but he would only ever talk of the good times—usually of amusing things that had happened. He would always make light of anything that might have been deemed extraordinary, and certainly eschewed anything suggesting that his service was heroic.

My research into his untold story has brought many invaluable rewards that I could not have ever imagined when I started this journey, and I will be forever grateful for the experience. I believe, however, that it still pales in comparison to what I might have gained from knowing the man as he grew older and even wiser. I am rueful for that alone, but I take solace in what I have learned and the rich experience of meeting so many connected people along the way. I have had some describe this quest, in tones ranging from commendation to rebuke, as a search for my father, and I have, at times, described it the same. Somewhere along the path, however, I came to a truly cathartic realization: he never really left me.

GLOSSARY

abort	multiple hole latrine in POW camp
Abwehr	German military intelligence service
ack-ack	antiaircraft artillery (see also, flak)
AG	Air Gunner
Appell	role call in German POW camp.
big city	Berlin
Blighty	the United Kingdom
boffin	scientist or technician who worked on development
bollocks	expletive used to connote contempt or annoyance
brass hat	ranks of Wing Commander and higher
Brid	Bridlington, port/fishing/vacation town in East Yorkshire
brown jobs	the army
brown off	to make unhappy or to frustrate
Burton, go for a	KIA (Killed in Action) on operations (see also, chop)
Canuck	a Canadian
CAVU	Ceiling and Visibility Unrestricted, clear conditions for flying
chit	written notice of transgression (see also, fizzer)

chop	KIA (Killed in Action), or simply FTR (Failed to Return) on operations hence "got the chop" (see also, "gone for a Burton")
chuffed	very happy, ecstatic
circuits and bumps	pilot training with landing and immediate take off
clapped out	tired, worn out, or nearing the end of useful life
clock	the clock is jargon for the aircraft altimeter (measures altitude)
CO	Commanding Officer
`com	onboard aircraft intercom
coned	intersection of several searchlights on one air-borne target
corkscrew	evasive maneuver, a diving turn to either port or starboard followed by climbing turn in opposite direction and repeated
D-bar	chocolate bar of superior quality often enclosed in American Red Cross parcels
do	an event or occurrence
`drome	aerodrome, air base
duff	bad, worthless
erk	groundcrew
feather	to turn a variable pitch propeller on a non-working engine so that the blades make minimum drag
ferret	German POW guard trained in escape detection
fizzer	disciplinary charge (see also, chit)
flak	antiaircraft artillery, derived from German, *Flugabwehrkanone*. (see also, ack-ack)
flaming onion	German antiaircraft artillery tracer shell
Flight	Flight Commander (see also, Skew-ell)
FTR	Failed to Return, KIA (killed in Action) or missing on operations (see also, chop or Burton)

FW 190	single engine German fighter made by Focke-Wulf
gen	information/news. Could be pukka (good) or duff (bad/questionable)
gong	a military medal
goon	uncomplimentary term for a guard in a German POW Camp
Halifax, Hallie, Halibag	four-engine Allied heavy bomber built by Handley-Page
Happy Valley	the heavily defended Ruhr Valley in Germany
HCU	Heavy Conversion Unit. Training unit where bomber crews transitioned from two-engine bombers to four-engine
HE	High Explosive, usually amatol
intel	Intelligence or Intelligence Section/Officer
ITS	Initial Training School
jammy	lucky or fluky in British slang
jankers	put on charge for military discipline violation
jerry	derogatory slang for a German (see also, Kraut, or hun)
juice	aviation fuel (see also, petrol)
kite	generic term for any aircraft
kriegie	Allied Prisoner of War, from German *Kriegsgefangener* (see also, POW)
LAC	Leading Aircraftman, junior rank in RAF and RCAF
Lancaster, Lanc	four-engine Allied heavy bomber built by Avro
line shoot	any narrative that might be perceived as exaggerating one's exploits (see also, shooting a line)
Link Trainer	early ground-based flight simulator
LMF	Lack of Moral Fibre. A likely stress-related inability to continue on operations

Mae West	inflatable life vest worn over flight suit
Manning Depot	initial RCAF station where new recruits learned the basics of military life
Me109	single engine German fighter made by Messerschmitt
Merlin	Rolls-Royce engine that powered Lancaster and early marks of Halifax bombers (I and II)
Mosquito	two-engine Allied fighter/bomber made by de Havilland (see also, mossie)
mossie	de Havilland Mosquito two-engine fighter-bomber
muckety-muck	high ranking officer (see also, brass hat)
NBG	No Bloody Good, unsatisfactory
operation, op	bombing assignment (see also, sortie)
OTU	Operational Training Unit where crews were formed and aircrew teamwork was honed
Oxford	Two-engine training aircraft made by Airspeed
P/O	Pilot Officer, lowest commissioned rank in RAF and RCAF
pack up	quit, stop working (see also, unserviceable or U/S)
Perspex	acrylic glass, trade name (Plexiglass)
petrol	aviation fuel (see also, juice)
PFF	Path Finder Force, target marking squadrons of RAF Bomber Command
piece of cake	something relatively easy
pontoon	card game with similarities to blackjack
POW	Prisoner of War (see also, *kriegie*)
prang	a crash, an attack, a bombing
pukka	good, accurate
put the wind up	making one nervous or anxious
RAF	Royal Air Force

RCAF	Royal Canadian Air Force
RN	Royal Navy
ropey	unsatisfactory, such as a ropey do
scarecrow shell	a purported German antiaircraft artillery shell that when detonated at altitude was said to have the appearance of an exploding aircraft. No corroborating evidence has ever been found for the existence of such a device.
second dickey	a co-pilot of an RAF bomber as part of his indoctrination to operational flying
shaky do	dangerous operation or occurrence
shooting a line	any narrative that might be perceived as exaggerating one's exploits (see also, line shoot)
Skew-ell	Squadron Leader, (usual rank of Flight Commander)
skirt	woman (see also bird)
SNAFU	acronym for Situation Normal All Fouled Up (or less euphemistically for the "F")
SOP	Standard Operating Procedure
sortie	bombing assignment (see also, operation)
SP	Service Police
spare bod	aircrewman not attached to a regular crew
sprog	relatively new or inexperienced
SqIntO	Squadron Intelligence Officer
Stalag	German POW camp. Shortened from German *Kriegsgefangenen-Mannschafts-Stammlager. Stalag Luft* were camps dedicated to captured aircrew
stooging	to idle around, in a flight circuit or over a target
T.I.	target Indicator, dropped by PFF these flares, in a variety of colours, marked the aiming point for the main bombing force

tracer	bullets or cannon projectiles that travel with a visible path to aid accuracy in shooting
Truppenlager	POW camp guard barracks
U/S	cease working, pronounced "yu ess" (see also, unserviceable or pack up)
unserviceable	cease working (see also, U/S or pack up)
Very pistol/cartridge	signal flare used for IFF (Identification Friend or Foe)
Vorlager	main German portion of the POW camp housing administration hospital and other such buildings
W/Op	Wireless Operator (pronounced "wop")
WAAF	Women's Auxiliary Air Force
Wellington	two-engine Allied medium bomber made by Vickers. (see also, Wimpy)
Wimpy	Vickers Wellington two-engine bomber
wingco	Wing Commander (usual rank of the Squadron Commander)
wire-happy	POW who is mentally or emotionally afflicted by internment
wizard, wizzo	excellent, very good
WO2	Warrant Officer, second grade
Yank	an American

CPSIA information can be obtained
at www.ICGtesting.com
Printed in the USA
BVHW080942230323
661008BV00006B/234

9 781525 520372